Dave -
From another
Canadian !
Enjoy.

# The Wrong Side of Right

by

## Tom Gosinski

ISBN-13  978-1484991312
ISBN-10  1484991311

Title ID:  4286729

CreateSpace, North Charleston, SC

Cover art by Karen Phillips

Printed in the United States of America

www.gosinski.com
Contact: Tom@gosinski.com

Woof Publishing LLC

*Happiness can exist only in acceptance.*
George Orwell

# Prologue
## August 2008

That morning dawned warm and humid in western Nebraska. Late-season flowers, their color depleted by the heat, lay in expectation of the scorching mid-day sun. The gentle rhythm of water running over the small, rock waterfall in the far corner of the yard filled the air with tranquility.

I drank my coffee in the screened patio—a very common protection in Nebraska built to keep out West-Nile-fever-carrying mosquitoes—and checked overnight e-mails. The state's largest daily journal, *The Omaha World Herald*, no longer delivered papers to the western portion of the state, so I also intended to read articles from online news outlets.

Doorbell chimes and the solid rapping of knuckles at the front entrance shattered my solitude. Because I wasn't anticipating company, I hadn't dressed to receive guests. With some embarrassment, I headed for the door in gym shorts and a T-shirt. Anyone who showed up without calling first got what they got.

The form of a man appeared through the bevels of the door's glass, but it was an unfamiliar figure. I opened the door, and before I could offer a greeting, the man introduced himself and presented a business card.

"Howard. Are you Tom?"

"I am."

A quick glance at the man's card showed an Arizona area code. Without thinking, I extended my hand, gave a polite shake, and invited him into my living room.

"Would you like a cup of coffee?"

"No, thank you."

I drained my cup and set it on the end table.

"You're a hard man to find." He studied me, perhaps for a reaction.

"Obviously not. You're here."

We sized each other up while red flags descended on my mind like ticker tape on a parade in Times Square.

Smith made a host of obligatory comments. "Beautiful morning." "This seems like a nice town." "Did you grow up here?"

I answered all with a formal "yes" or a less-than-committed "uh huh."

With unexpected suddenness, his generalities changed to specifics. "Tom, do you know the McCains?"

"Of course, I do. Who doesn't? Who do you work for, Howard?" The ticker tape almost blinded me.

"I'm retired from the FBI, Tom, and I've been hired by some people to locate you and ask some questions about the McCains."

"What people? Are they Democrats or Republicans?"

"It's not a name I knew prior to being hired, and I know it's not a name you would know. I tried googling it and found nothing."

At face value the man seemed harmless, but his lack of straight answers suggested otherwise. I had learned the hard way to trust my gut instincts.

"Howard, you mean you can't tell me who signs your checks?" The ticker tape slammed into my skull as though driven by gale-force winds. "You understand I'm not going to answer any questions, especially from a guy who can't tell me who he works for." Pregnant pauses make me uncomfortable.

It was time for the meeting to end. "Look, Howard, I'm sorry you traveled all the way from Arizona to find me. Maybe you should have just called." I got up from the sofa and headed toward the front door. He followed. I felt bad for him because he had to go back to his employer empty-handed, but not bad enough to give him what he wanted. Instinctively, I again extended my hand. "It was nice meeting you, Howard."

"If you decide you do want to talk to me, Tom, please call. I'd be happy to come back to Nebraska." His pleading tone did nothing to change my mind.

I forced a smile. "Please, don't hold your breath. Next time, call first."

After closing the door, I wondered why I'd gone through the motions of ending our conversation with a handshake and the socially acceptable "nice meeting you." It hadn't been nice at all.

The McCains and their drama had landed at my front door. Fifteen years had passed since I last confronted issues regarding John and Cindy McCain, and I hoped that chapter of my life would remain in the past. The fact that my hope might be in vain had already reared its head in the form of calls from several national and international news agencies, inquiring about my relationship with the McCains and wanting to know if I could add anything to the discussion about their background.

I live in a small town, so I called my friend Scott, the sole City Attorney, and told him about Howard's visit.

"I know all about it," he informed me. "He stopped at the police station and was asking questions about you." Scott went on to tell me that Mark, the chief of police, had called him and brought him up to date on Howard's visit.

"What should I do if anybody else shows up?" I asked.

"Tell them to call me. If that doesn't get them off your steps, call Mark."

I ended the call with a smile of relief. Although his law practice was small and located in a rural community, I didn't doubt Scott's ability. Furthermore, I could ask him to involve the police if I ever felt harassed. Mark was a good guy, too. I wouldn't hesitate to call him if I needed him.

I hadn't planned anything for the day, so I headed for the tranquility of my garden.

Gardening had become my passion. I was recovering from twenty-seven weeks of chemotherapy, and two months had passed since my final chemo appointment. Although I felt good, I still wasn't one-hundred percent. My oncologist, while excited by my progress, encouraged me to pace myself through my recovery. I had followed his advice to avoid over-exertion and reduce stress. Gardening provided the perfect remedy for my unexpected morning encounter.

As with everything else, however, I wanted my garden to be perfect, so it wasn't without its stresses. It's possible to manipulate plants and, to a point, even train them. But in nature, control is limited. Had someone told me that before I decided to make gardening a hobby, I might have picked another kind of relaxation.

Never in my life had I been *really* ill, so the previous fall, when I fell sick, my life changed. I had been working hard all summer; therefore, it didn't seem strange that I was continually tired. No aches, pains, or nausea suggested serious illness. At nearly fifty years of age, I thought, it's *a bitch getting old* and tried to pace myself accordingly. Finally, a friend—someone I didn't consider unduly sensitive—told me I sounded tired. I went to see a doctor. After a battery of tests and consultations with a variety of specialists, I learned that I had cancer. It was determined that the best course of action for my type of cancer would be an aggressive series of chemotherapy treatments.

Fortunately, my body tolerated the powerful, toxic drugs. Generally, the second or third day after my treatment, I felt nauseated within the first hour of arising. After that, I was fine.

Going to chemotherapy didn't bother me because, with each treatment, I felt better. My routine included taking a stack of magazines, my iPod, a Jimmy John turkey sandwich, and a glass of lemonade to each of my chemo appointments, where I stretched out in a recliner in the Infusion Room. A small, special group of nurses worked with the cancer patients, so, other than the needle in my arm and the bag of orange-soda-colored liquid that dripped the toxic potion into my body, the afternoons at chemotherapy provided a pleasant diversion.

My good friend Julie was diagnosed with cancer within a months of my diagnosis. When possible, we scheduled "chemo dates" and got adjoining cubicles, where we spent the afternoon talking and laughing. My treatment didn't take as long as hers, but once my needle was removed, I often stayed with her until her treatment was done.

Julie's body didn't respond to the drugs as mine did.

I survived.

Julie died.

Gardening provided me ample time for relaxation and contemplation. By day's end, after lots of weed pulling and dead-heading blooms, I knew I had to control the situation by entering the debate about the McCains…on *my* terms.

# Chapter 1

The first time I met Cindy McCain, I was surprised by her youth. I had met her husband, John, the Senator, and I knew his wife was younger—I just didn't know they were decades apart in age. At the time I thought her to be in her mid- to late-thirties; the Senator had to be in his sixties.

Cindy's blonde hair, cut in a sporty yet sophisticated style with a silver-gray stripe in her bangs, accentuated her tall, athletically feminine figure. Her beautifully tailored, ivory pantsuit trimmed in black, gold buttons at the cuff, didn't convey the overdone pretense of many of Phoenix's well-to-do women. Her simple jewelry—a Cartier Love Bracelet, a Rolex, and a ring set with large sapphires and diamonds—completed the look. Upon closer observation, I noted the heaviness of her makeup and her chewed, unpolished fingernails. These seemed incongruous with her otherwise elegant appearance.

The occasion was a meeting in the Government and International Affairs offices of America West Airlines in early 1991. She had requested the meeting to appeal to America West for assistance in transporting her and members of a non-profit organization she had founded, the American Voluntary Medical Team (AVMT), to Kuwait at the end of the still-being-waged, first Gulf War, "Operation Desert Storm." My position as a manager in that office dictated my presence.

Cindy had started AVMT to address the medical needs of victims of natural disasters, impoverished areas, and wars. In Kuwait she hoped to assist victims of the Gulf War.

America West didn't fly to the gulf, but its 747s were under contract with the United States government, specifically, the Department of Defense (DOD), to transport troops to and from friendly countries neighboring Kuwait. From those neighboring countries, the U.S. military would transport its troops. After the war, America West's 747s would travel to the region empty so they could carry troops out of the area and back to the States. Most major U.S. carriers participate in these wartime airlifts because of the profitability of the contracts.

My boss, Marty, Senior VP of Legal and General Counsel to the airline, ran the meeting. In addition to Cindy, it was attended by two of her colleagues, Kathy and Barbara. Neither woman added much to the discussion, so I assumed they were there to suggest the appearance of a well-staffed organization.

By the end of the meeting, Marty and I understood Cindy's request, and I believe she and her helpers understood that, because America West planes were being chartered by an agency of the U.S. government, we couldn't promise AVMT volunteers space onboard. The Department of Defense would decide whether or not to allow the AVMT on the flights to the gulf region.

Cindy appeared confident in stating that her husband's office would be willing to assist us in every way possible to make the trip happen and, if need be, the Senator himself would make calls on our behalf. The meeting ended with all the necessary and appropriate suggestions of our willingness to assist the AVMT and our offer to get back to Cindy's associates with regular updates on our progress.

\* \* \* \* \*

"So, what do you think?" Marty asked after the coterie had left the conference room.

"She's pretty," I said.

"That's not what I mean." He lifted one corner of his mouth and gave me his signature smile.

"I know," I answered. "It sounds kind of crazy to me. But fun."

Marty dipped his head so he could look at me over the top of his glasses. "Let's see what we can do."

Over the next several weeks, as the war in Kuwait continued, Marty made many calls to DOD representatives who negotiated the charters. There seemed little chance they would agree to allow civilians onboard a DOD charter and fly them into a war region. However, with the promised assistance of John McCain's office, doors opened and meaningful discussions began. Marty took a deep, professional interest in the project. Because of his tenacity, a deal was finally struck that allowed ordinary citizens—AVMT volunteers—to fly on America West's DOD-chartered planes to the gulf.

Of course, because the DOD didn't want to be liable for the safety of non-military individuals traveling to the gulf, a letter of indemnity had to be agreed upon, relieving the DOD of any responsibility. That letter, drafted by Marty and approved by the DOD, had to be signed by each person who intended to travel with the organization.

Marty skillfully jumped all the hurdles put before him and, I'm sure, was pleased with himself and his work. I know he anticipated that his hard work would be properly noticed by one of the airline's most important advocates, Senator John McCain.

Cindy and her staff had put together a team of forty-some doctors, nurses, support staff, and members of the media to make the trip to Kuwait. Because the team was made up of volunteers who would be taking time away from work at considerable personal expense, Marty had me work with other airlines to provide free and reduced travel for the return portion of the trip. The DOD allowed AVMT to fly the outbound portion of the trip, its chartered flight from Phoenix, to a military base in Saudi Arabia, at no expense to AVMT or its volunteers.

Over the next several weeks, I attended several of the organization's planning meetings and worked closely with AVMT staff to determine the amount of equipment and supplies that needed to be transported to the gulf. The team amassed a huge amount of supplies—cases of food and water, medical equipment and supplies, and pharmaceutical drugs necessary for a variety of clinics and surgeries—as well as personal luggage and bedding. It was an enormous undertaking, and the AVMT staff seemed tested by the sheer volume of the task.

The meetings were held at the McCain's home—Cindy's childhood home—which, I understand, her parents had given her and she completely remodeled. The estate on Phoenix's Central Avenue sat on a corner in the middle of a neighborhood filled with large, older homes. A stucco and iron fence surrounded it. Gates on the south and east sides of the property provided entry to the massive, single-story, stucco structure capped with terra cotta shingles. The exterior of the house was picture perfect.

I was startled by the contrast between the exterior of the home and its interior. Inside, the stucco walls were painted an unattractive ivory gloss. The first time I visited the house, the entry area was stacked with boxes of varying sizes and shapes, and the walls were cluttered with pictures. I like family photographs, but, like everything, I think they should be displayed in moderation. There were so many pictures, so many things to look at, that it was impossible to take them all in. I thought, "Edit, edit, edit." The disparity between the exterior and interior reminded me of the incongruousness between Cindy's ill-kept nails and excessive makeup and her exquisitely elegant suit when I first met her. Looking back now, I realize that something didn't seem quite right in either case, but that didn't register at the time.

The living room, where we congregated, was furnished with willow chairs and sofas with multi-colored cushions. Cindy told me the furniture had been built by Arizona crafts-men and, although I appreciated the sentiment of its origins, I found it uncomfortable. The room was accessorized with elephants of all materials, sizes, and shapes. I assumed that was the McCains' nod to the GOP. Juxtaposed oddly to the elephants was a collection of Kachina dolls. Either collection might have been interesting singularly, but together . . . I don't know. Once again, the incongruity nudged at me.

After several organizational meetings, the team was formed, its supplies were in place, all the legal issues were remedied, and travel to and from the gulf region was final-ized. At one of our last meetings, Cindy invited me to travel with them to handle logistics and expedite the team's move-ment through all the various airport facilities they would be encountering.

I'd not anticipated an invitation, so my first internal reac-tion was "No." I tried to act appreciative while contemplat-ing everything I'd have to do to prepare for the trip. Cindy seemed confused that I didn't jump at the opportunity—I doubt many people ever told her no—and the excitement in her voice seemed to subside.

"Tom, if you don't think it's possible, I'll understand." she said.

"It's not that I don't want to go but I'll have to take vaca-tion time, clear my desk, get someone to watch my apart-ment . . ."

"I'm sure Marty will give you time off."

I wasn't as sure as she seemed to be. We'd been very busy in our office, and, if I were to be gone, my work would need to be passed on to somebody else who would no doubt have an equally full plate. Also, I'd used up my vacation time, so I'd have to take unpaid vacation time. Making that kind of sacrifice for AVMT hadn't been part of my agenda.

Feeling as though I'd disappointed Cindy by not saying yes, I watched her move away from me and involve herself in the sales of AVMT shirts. She joked with people about their shirt sizes—making what seemed to me to be subtle, mean-spirited jokes about peoples' sizes and body shapes—and appeared to enjoy making people feel self-conscious.

Other members of the team asked me a variety of questions. It seemed the nervousness of traveling into a war zone intimated many of them. Most of the questions had been addressed in our group discussions. However, I knew we needed everyone to be confident in their decisions to make the trip, so I was happy to answer all of them again.

Personally, I had mixed feelings about the trip. Glad that I could use work as a reason for not making an immediate decision, I mulled over the intriguing idea of going to Kuwait. The notion of traveling with people I barely knew didn't appeal to me. Also, given the size of Cindy's personal entourage—Kathy, Barbara, Jeri, Keri (Jeri's granddaughter), and photographer Ken—I wasn't sure my contribution would be sufficient to make my participation worthwhile. However, as people asked me questions about the travel arrangements and documents, it became apparent to me that no one from Cindy's staff was prepared to handle these matters. My participation might be of benefit after all.

I believed the invitation somehow rewarded me for my work, but since it was part of my job duties at America West to work with Arizona's congressional delegation, I couldn't quite accept that the work I had done for AVMT warranted the invitation. After deciding it opened the door to a once-in-a-lifetime opportunity and something I would cherish forever, I discussed it with Marty and asked if I could take two weeks unpaid vacation time to accompany AVMT to Kuwait. Marty insisted that my accompanying the team and "assisting Mrs. McCain" would be of benefit to the airline's relationship with Senator McCain. He also told me he didn't think the trip would be a vacation, so it would not be unpaid.

"Represent us well," he said.

In mid-April, just three days after finalizing the trip plans, we were scheduled to depart. Cindy held an evening meeting to brief the group and ensure that everyone had completed all the necessary paperwork and possessed a current passport.

AVMT had ordered shirts in white or red with the AVMT logo embroidered on the chest for team members to buy. Without exception, everyone had purchased several shirts, so I knew that it would be easy to identify and corral them during the trip despite my not knowing them well.

I'd had the flight manifest identifying the travelers for a few weeks, so it was fun to meet people and put faces to names. The diversity of the group members surprised me—doctors and nurses (young and old), a medical student, non-medical thrill-seekers, and even a jeweler—and I looked forward to knowing each of them. I spoke to the group about the departure time, documents, and carry-on bag restrictions, and I provided answers to a variety of questions about the flights. We confirmed the departure time and everyone went on their way.

When I arrived at the gate the evening of our departure, I was surprised by the size of the crowd. Of course, it was easy to pick out the travelers—they were wearing the AVMT shirts. I assumed the rest of the crowd consisted of spouses and children. I think all the local television stations had sent news crews, and it appeared all of them were in line to interview Cindy. I don't recall that Senator McCain was there. It was a weeknight, so he have been in Washington.

Getting the plane boarded for our departure to Saudi Arabia wasn't unlike rounding up a group of excited school kids for a field trip. The spring of 1991 was pre-9/11, so family members and friends were allowed to accompany passengers to departure gates. Their presence heightened the air of enthusiasm, and the addition of television crews and flash of bulbs from personal cameras created a Hollywood-like atmosphere.

I had spent most of the day ensuring that all the medical equipment and supplies AVMT had obtained were properly inventoried and loaded on pallets for easy, efficient transport. By the time I reached the departure gate, corralling the volunteers seemed more than a little challenging. I understood the excitement and emotion of the moment and knew that once we were all onboard and the volunteers had found their seats, things would settle down.

Because of the size of the 747 and the relatively small passenger load, our entourage was able to claim individual rows of seats and stretch out during the flight. With the exception of a short stop to refuel in Europe, the flight to Saudi Arabia proceeded without interruption. It provided many members of the team an opportunity to become acquainted, watch a movie, play a card game, or catch up on sleep. I spent time answering questions about the logistics of baggage movement, document processing, and the return flights. I don't know if it was a sense of homesickness or a dawning of reality about the nature of the adventure that made people think about their trip home.

During the flight I spent several hours visiting with Cindy about all kinds of things—her children, her parents, how she had met her husband, and what her long-term goals were for AVMT. In our conversations, she referred to Keri,

Jeri's granddaughter, as her daughter. However, I assumed she must be her cousin's daughter and possibly they had an odd way of referring to family members. Keri and Cindy seemed to have distance between them—they didn't speak to each other very often, nor did Keri sit with Cindy. It seemed odd, but I wasn't comfortable enough in my position to question Cindy, Jeri, Keri, or even Kathy about the specifics of the relationship.

Regardless, I hadn't spent any one-on-one time with Cindy, so I appreciated the opportunity to get acquainted. She seemed personable, and our conversation flowed naturally. But I had a sense that her comments were rehearsed and shared freely with others. Just as I had in our initial meeting at America West, I noted her habit of using her index fingers to pick at her thumb nails. Maybe because we were in a more relaxed environment, she didn't hide her other habit of chewing her nails. To me, it was an odd juxtaposition to see her Cartier bracelet in close proximity to those horrible nails.

During the flight, I also became better acquainted with Kathy and Barbara, the women who had accompanied Cindy to our initial meeting, and another member of the group, Ken, a photographer who would document the group's mission through pictures. Ken told me he'd accompanied Cindy on other missions. My best guess was that they'd been traveling together for about five years and that he had a photographic history of AVMT.

I was obviously the new player within AVMT's inner circle. Nearly all the members seemed to want to tell me about their strong relationships with Cindy. Barbara, the one exception and most sophisticated of the lot, also appeared the most self-confident and least territorial. Kathy, the dutiful personal secretary, occupied herself with nonsensical busy work, and Jeri didn't so much remind me about her familial relationship with Cindy as she did her relationship with Cindy's parents, the Hensleys. Ken reinforced the strength of his relationship by telling tales of their previous adventures.

An uncomfortable feeling crept over me, then dissipated. I frowned. This was a different game. I didn't know the rules.

# Chapter 2

We landed at an airbase in Saudi Arabia and couldn't help but be impressed by the variety of aircraft and their sheer numbers. The runways were lined with various fighter jets. Behemoth C5 cargo planes and smaller C130s congested the tarmac closer to the hangars. Several airlines from the United States were represented by their 747s, painted in company colors and bearing the carriers' logos, presumably there to carry troops back to the States. Our plane taxied and parked among the 747s, and everyone onboard was allowed to disembark—personal belongings in tow—to stretch their legs and wait for the next segment of our trip.

The Saudi sun shone bright and strong, and the temperature on the tarmac had to be tens of degrees higher than in the areas beyond it. Unfortunately, we weren't allowed to leave the area, so we did what we could to find relief in whatever shade could be found. Most of us dropped our bags on the shady side of trucks and sat on them.

It didn't take long for the plane's cargo hatches to be opened and all the pallets of AVMT cargo to be off-loaded. I hadn't seen everything all together until then and was overwhelmed at the imposing mountain of supplies.

A military liaison introduced himself and told us the team and all its cargo would be flown into Kuwait City on a C130. I don't know much about military planes, but I understand the C130 to be the workhorse of the air fleet. It's not a sexy plane—its fuselage seems short and stubby, and the military paint scheme of drab green didn't do anything to make it sleeker. All our palletized supplies were wrapped in plastic, loaded on a conveyor system, accessed from a rear-loading ramp, and swallowed up by the plane.

We were told to collect our carry-on luggage and congregate at the back of the plane for boarding. As we boarded, we were each given a pair of disposable earplugs and directed to single rows of inward facing seats that lined the fuselage. We sat in metal, fold-down seats that were equipped with harnesses of the same drab green as the plane. Although the seats faced the center of the plane, we weren't able to see the people across from us because our sight line was blocked by the pallets of supplies. None of the aircraft's inner wiring was hidden behind panels, so the ceilings and walls were covered in an impressive array of wires and tubing.

It seemed we were all in strange territory. I didn't know whether any of the team's members had served in the military or flown in a C130. By the looks on their faces, I gathered that none of us felt at ease. Ken and Cindy always put on an air of "been there, done that," but I couldn't imagine any scenario that would have landed them in a situation like this. Like the rest of us, Cindy looked from side to side, trying to determine which harness was hers and which belonged to the travelers alongside her. For the first time, I saw a crack in her confidence—I doubt she'd ever been confronted with a spaghetti-like pile of restraints in First Class—but, as soon as one of the airmen showed her how to secure herself into the seat, she laughed at the others who struggled to get themselves secured.

Once all AVMT's cargo had been loaded, olive-colored netting was placed over it and secured to metal fittings in the floor. Shortly after the doors were closed and secured, the aircraft took off at a steep ascent. The military personnel who had joined us were more than happy to answer our many queries, and I was invited, along with Cindy, to climb up a ladder to view the cockpit. Because of the plane's design and the odd positioning of the cockpit, the forward view out the windows was amazing. The landscape across Saudi Arabia—at least from our view—didn't seem much different than some of Arizona's more remote desert regions.

Our flight to Kuwait City was short, maybe 30 or 40 minutes. The C130 wasn't insulated for sound so the noisy ride didn't invite conversation.

We couldn't appreciate our descent into Kuwait City because a C130 has no windows in its fuselage. When the tail of the aircraft opened, we were greeted by dark skies—despite the afternoon hour—and a rancid odor. Our plane had taxied to an area adjacent to the airport terminal. Although street lights and lights on the exterior of the terminal were illuminated, the atmosphere seemed strangely odd and surreal. As we disembarked, we realized the clouds over the airport weren't created by nature, but instead were thick, toxic clouds of smoke billowing from oil well fires surrounding the city.

"Damn it," I heard one of the nurses say as she wiped the back of her pants. "Don't sit down." The oil from the toxic clouds had settled on everything, including the concrete, benches in front of the terminal. After the nurse's exclamation, several team members stood and found the seats of their pants to be covered in a light layer of the dark residue.

All the AVMT cargo and members' personal luggage were loaded on large, military trucks, and the team members were told to take a fleet of unmanned Chevrolet Suburbans provided by the Kuwait Ministry of Health to our housing in Kuwait City, the SAS Hotel.

"Here you go. You drive." Cindy tossed me a set of keys.

"Me? You sure? You've never ridden with me," I said with a chuckle.

Our maroon vehicle had the Ministry of Health's seal on the driver's and passenger's side doors. I don't know if I ever said it out loud, but it occurred to me that the seals provided the perfect bullseye for a left-behind Iraqi marksman. Cindy rode in the passenger seat. Ken, the photographer, Kathy, Barbara, and a doctor I hadn't yet met filled the second and third row bench seats.

The truck carrying our supplies and luggage led the caravan; the rest of us followed. I wished I'd not been driving—I would have preferred to be a spectator—but I was pleased that Cindy had asked me to command the vehicle.

The ride through Kuwait City was eye-opening . . . and slow. Bullet-ridden cars, collapsed buildings, and abandoned military equipment littered the landscape. Traffic was congested because of the many military checkpoints scattered throughout the city. A series of concrete barriers set on opposite sides of the roads demanded that traffic slow to maneuver the zigzag patterns. Both U.S. and Kuwaiti troops manned the checkpoints, but many of the Kuwaiti troops appeared way too young to be carrying the guns slung over their shoulders.

U.S. troops were pleasant, but it was impossible to understand the Kuwaitis' questions. However, they waved us on when we flashed our passports.

When we arrived at the SAS Hotel, we were startled to find it abandoned and its doors and windows open to the elements. Neither water nor electricity appeared to be functioning.

The hotel was situated on Kuwait City's shoreline and had great views of the gulf. However, directly in front of the hotel, dug into the sand beaches, were the rotatable artillery guns that the Iraqi army had placed there in anticipation of a water invasion. Cases of live ammunition stood like sentinels around the weapons.

The solemnity of the day was broken as many of us climbed onto the big guns and had our picture taken. Like everything else in Kuwait City, the sand beaches, the artillery guns, and all the other horizontal surfaces at the SAS were covered in a layer of black, oily residue from the oil well fires.

*　*　*　*　*

Back at the SAS, we identified several reasonably clean rooms that opened onto a courtyard and began to offload our supplies from the military truck. We formed a human chain and passed the cases of food and water to the room farthest from the unloading area. We had begun to unload the rest of the supplies into a second room when one of our military escorts informed us that we would be moving to another location. The SAS wasn't properly secured. Our safety couldn't be guaranteed.

After everything was reloaded onto the truck, our caravan traveled through more roadblocks and debris until we arrived at a small hospital on the far side of the city. Even though it was early evening, we were all tired from two days of traveling and shuffling. The enthusiasm for unloading the trucks had passed.

The hospital, a one-story, brick structure punctuated by slim, vertical windows spaced about fifteen feet apart, was similar to those built in small towns in the Midwest during the 1960s. With its speckled, vinyl-tiled floors and long, florescent light fixtures in the halls, it was a huge step up from the SAS Hotel. We were given an empty wing of the T-shaped building, and, in addition to comfortable hospital beds, we enjoyed adequate bathroom and shower facilities.

That night, we prepared some of the food we had transported from the States—as I recall, we ate canned chicken with barbeque sauce—and everyone retired early. It had been two days since anyone had seen a real bed and, although the promise of a night's sleep seemed attractive, the environment in which we were to sleep was, to say the least, less than comforting. Everyone in the group seemed mildly irritable but all seemed to accept the realities of our situation. Cindy's overconfident exterior seemed to diminish to a more realistic level and, while others seemed to form bonds, Cindy, in my opinion, withdrew from the group. I believe she felt burdened by her responsibilities for the group, but her withdrawal seemed to conflict with her leadership role. She depended on Kathy and Barbara's assistance in preparing her bed and fetching her meals and looked to Ken to bolster her spirits. I also was of support to Cindy in arranging the transportation of people and supplies—a logistics person of sorts—and was included in various decisions that were to be made about how AVMT might be best utilized.

That night, the reality of our mission to Kuwait hit me. We were in the midst of a war-torn city and didn't seem to have any direction. I'd assumed the AVMT staff had made specific plans for the group, but as the trip progressed, I realized we were flying by the seat of our pants. Oddly to me, those who'd traveled with AVMT in the past didn't seem bothered by the absence of a well-thought-out plan.

Our first day in Kuwait City proved neither eventful nor productive. Much of the day was spent trying to determine where AVMT services would be of greatest benefit. Given the overall disorganization of the city and its medical facilities, as well as the difficulty in identifying people who might be able to give us direction, we experienced much confusing back-and-forth between our host hospital and the Sheraton Hotel, where a variety of government officials and news organizations were housed.

Late that afternoon, Ken entered our shared room. "Let's go take some pictures." He grabbed his backpack and a camera. I was eager to see more of Kuwait City, so I grabbed my backpack, too, and closed the door behind us as we left.

"You think it'll be okay with Cindy?" I asked.

"Hell, yeah. It's her idea."

I saw her waiting for us at the end of the hall. She was carrying her backpack.

"Hey, Tom. Are you gonna drive?" she asked.

I shrugged my shoulders. "Sure. I'll drive."

The three of us got into the Suburban and left the hospital.

"You think they'll miss us?" Ken asked.

"Who cares?" Cindy replied.

I remained silent throughout our tour of the city, only asking questions about directions. Taken aback by Ken's casual, sometimes colorful vocabulary, I was surprised he would use such language in front of Cindy. However, it soon became apparent they were old friends, as they shared many adventures they had experienced together on previous AVMT trips.

At some security checkpoints, aggressive soldiers pointed their guns in the windows while they checked our passports. At others we were waved through the mazes of concrete barricades without even having to present our papers.

The neighborhoods we drove through were unlike any I'd ever seen. Many buildings had been bombed. Others had port-window-size holes through which shells had passed without exploding. The degree of destruction varied widely; some places didn't appear to have been touched while others were totally devastated. I've not served in the military, so I was totally unprepared for such sights.

On occasion, we stopped the vehicle and went into the half-standing buildings to see the damaged interiors. In corners and closets of several buildings, we discovered piles of fist-sized, hard-crusted buns we later learned were rations that had belonged to the Iraqi soldiers. One would think the bread would have spoiled or molded, but because of the hardness of the crust, it appeared to have been preserved in the desert conditions. Still, it's hard to imagine military leaders sending their soldiers into war with hard-crusted buns for sustenance.

I reeled at the appalling sights, but Cindy appeared to take most of them in stride. As AVMT's official photographer, Ken did what he did best—he took pictures, lots of them. I thought a photographic history of the organization's mission was a great idea, but I was surprised that most of his pictures were of Cindy and or the environment. I don't recall many that included the volunteer team members whose skills and willingness to give freely of their time made this mission possible.

When we returned to the hospital later that afternoon, Kathy appeared troubled that we had not included her in our excursion. Her ongoing questions and suggestions that "everyone" was concerned over our whereabouts became a little disconcerting.

"Where'd you go?" she asked.

"For a ride." Cindy responded without making eye contact.

"We didn't know where you went."

No one responded.

"What'd you see?"

Cindy either didn't hear or ignored the question.

"Hey, Tom, can you hand me that bag?" Ken asked as he headed away from the uncomfortable confrontation.

"I have it." The two of us retreated to the relative quiet of our room.

In addition to Kathy and Barbara, Cindy's aunt, Jeri, and Keri had accompanied AVMT to Kuwait. Maybe sixteen or seventeen years old and petite like her grandmother, Keri seemed out of place on a mission to a war-torn area. In fact, I never understood why she had been permitted to travel with the group. This didn't seem to me to be a safe place for anyone who didn't have business there. I also wondered why Cindy required so many assistants in addition to our abundance of non-medical volunteers. Still, her staff seemed to busy themselves with a variety of tasks.

Everyone shared responsibility for meal preparation. Meals consisted of every kind of canned meat and vegetables, pita bread, health bars, candy that didn't melt, and nuts. Cindy and her staff managed the inventory of supplies.

I don't know how old Jeri was, but I assumed she was near retirement age. A well-tanned, petite woman who couldn't have exceeded five feet by more than an inch or two, she, like Barbara, was a "decided" blonde. Between her "busy" jobs, she took cigarette "breaks" many times a day. Keri appeared quite reserved, and I imagined her—because of her youth— to be overwhelmed by the experience. At the same time, she was a teenager, so she may have been bored. Regardless of the reason for her apparent reservation, she didn't interact much with me. I never had the opportunity to become acquainted with her.

On our second full day in Kuwait City, we gained traction. Our doctors and nurses received assignments to different hospitals throughout the city where their various areas of expertise could be best used to benefit the population. One doctor, a surgeon, had a very full slate of procedures. I watched him operate on an Iraqi soldier, a prisoner whose leg had been mutilated by a land mine. Because of the loose protocol in the hospitals, I was able to put on scrubs and a mask, enter the operating room, and observe.

The soldier, a tall man with a dark, full beard, was already under anesthesia when I entered. White sheets draped his body, and his eyelids had been taped shut to keep them from opening involuntarily during the surgery—a practice I found disconcerting. The starkness of the white tape against his dark skin created an eerie feeling of a Hollywood thriller movie set.

From mid-thigh down, his legs were exposed. Small, crater-like openings caused by hot shrapnel as it tore through his skin ran the length of his legs. The small wounds weren't of great concern, I learned, because the heat of the shrapnel cauterized the blood vessels as it came in contact with them.

The man's leg had to be removed just below the knee. The doctor cut the skin below the point where it would actually be sawed off. The excess skin, white from the lack of blood, was turned back onto the knee. My stomach turned as the blade hummed its way through bone. Once the leg had been cut and removed and all the vessels properly sealed, the skin was pulled down over the stub, drawn tight, gathered, and sewn shut.

To my surprise, I felt no emotion about the man's losing his leg. Other than my initial reaction to the sound of the blade, I wasn't revolted, perhaps because I was far removed from my comfort zone. Or maybe I was overwhelmed by everything I'd witnessed. Whatever the reason, the surgery struck me as very clinical. My mind seemed numbed and my senses overloaded—the type of reaction attributed to excessive stimulation. For the first time in my life, I was without feeling.

Over the next several days, I watched a number of surgeries, but none was as memorable as that of the Iraqi soldier. Unique and unexpected as this entire experience was, I wondered whether I would have signed on with America West had my job description included observer of surgeries in the war-torn Middle East—or anywhere else, for that matter. Perhaps not…

Early one morning, several days into the trip, I answered a knock at my door and opened it to find a very animated Cindy standing there.

"We're going to a refugee camp." She practically bubbled over with excitement.

"What?"

"We're going to the Safwan refugee camp in southern Iraq to take care of the sick and wounded."

"How're we getting there?"

"Driving," she answered.

I forced down the trepidation rising in my throat. "Who's going?"

"I'm working on that. You'd better start packing."

I retreated into my room and threw some clothes in my backpack. She said we would travel light because we would be away for only a few days.

Ken arrived in the room, obviously stoked by the prospects of the refugee camp. "This is the real shit," he announced.

He had a mess kit, a huge knife fixed to his belt, a fatigue-type vest with pockets for everything, a compass, rolls of film, battery packs—all sorts of things I never considered. Obviously, he had come better prepared for this kind of excursion than I had. He told me he'd never been in the military, his present enthusiasm suggested a wannabe scenario.

We met Cindy at the Suburban, and I was surprised to find that few people would be traveling with us. Cindy, Ken, a few doctors, a couple of nurses, and I were the only ones making the trip. The rest of the AVMT group would carry on in Kuwait City.

Excitement ran through the small group, although I wasn't quite sure why. As volunteer service providers, we were, in my opinion, ill prepared to make such a dangerous trip—and my gut instinct told me that it was a hazardous undertaking.

Escorted by two military vehicles, we traveled on Highway 80 out of Kuwait City. I wasn't familiar with the road's official name, but I was very aware of its infamous nickname: The Highway of Death. Like any interstate highway in the States, it was a four-lane highway that stretched from Kuwait City to Basrah. Unlike the highways in the U.S., however, the traffic wasn't moving. All four lanes of the super highway were strewn with empty vehicles of every kind, military and civilian. Some sat on the concrete ribbons, others scattered onto the road's shoulders.

This was the stretch of highway where Iraqi soldiers fleeing Kuwait City and the U.S. invasion had been caught dead in their tracks, literally—hence its nickname. We parked, walked the metal graveyard, and returned to the Suburban. It was hard to imagine the military might that caused this devastation and even tougher to comprehend the fear that the fleeing Iraqis must have experienced. Undoubtedly, the scene had seemed to them an Armageddon.

As we continued our trek to Safwan, we were instructed to drive in clear, fresh tire tracks. Our military liaison cautioned that Iraqi troops had placed land mines all over Kuwait and driving through fresh tires tracks would minimize our chances of hitting a land mine. Another wave of trepidation roared through my body, confirming my gut's assessment of this ill-advised venture. This was definitely *not* in my job description. Marty had been right—the trip to Kuwait could not in any way be construed as a vacation.

In stark contrast to the horror outside the Suburban, our conversation was fun, light, and tentative. I pushed aside the thought that others must be sharing my apprehension about the trip once we found a rock radio station. When other topics waned, it was easy to talk about the music.

I was awed by the sea of white tents we found on our arrival at the refugee camp. The Red Cross had a significant presence—the roofs of their tents distinguished by their bright red logo. A tall, barbed-wire fence encircled the tents, and entrances on each side of the camp were manned by U.S. military and United Nations troops.

Confusion surrounded our arrival. The guards at the entrances didn't appear to be expecting us, and the people they contacted didn't know what role we were to play. I must commend Cindy for her impressive skills and persistence in finding a place for us to settle and set up a triage station. She was determined AVMT would have a presence at the camp, but in hindsight I suspect she must have felt ill-prepared. The whole situation struck me as yet another example of the lack of a well-planned itinerary and appropriate preparation.

Thousands of refugees filled the camp. Our handful of people would be of limited benefit. Still, AVMT's triage processed many people—mostly women and children—suffering a plethora of symptoms related to the camp's conditions. Dehydration, lack of proper nutrition, and anxiety topped the list of ailments, but I sensed by the look in their eyes that many of the people we saw were suffering shock. Coming from the comforts of homes in the United States, it's impossible to imagine the horrors these people had experienced—or how they survived. Yet, they still possessed an air of determination.

When we left the refugee camp, we were given a military escort to a U.S. army camp that had been set up in the desert near Safwan. The small camp contained maybe 20 or 30 tents, and the soldiers in the camp were hospitable. I believe they enjoyed having outsiders as guests. We arrived late in the afternoon, and one of the first things they offered was use of their showers. The series of four or five wooden stalls—much like those on the television show, *MASH*—sat at the far end of the camp, just inside the perimeter barbed wire.

AVMT members took turns at the showers. Just after Cindy had started hers, the thwat, thwat, thwat sound of helicopter blades beating the air caught our attention. In the distance, three black choppers approached. Their menacing appearance made me wish I was home in Phoenix, and they obviously intended to land.

Soldiers raced around the camp, grabbing things that might be blown and protecting themselves from the tornado-like sand spirals. One of them ran to our tent and told us a general onboard one of the helicopters wanted to speak to Cindy as soon as they had landed.

Cindy headed across the camp from the showers, dressed in hospital scrubs, a towel around her head, carrying her clothes from the day.

She looked up at the helicopters. "Who's that?"

"It's a general. He's here to speak to you," someone replied.

Ducking into her tent, she reappeared in khakis and an AVMT shirt, her hair combed.

"Ok. Here we go." She headed toward the choppers.

After a few minutes, she returned, smiling and shaking her head. "Let's get packed and load up the Suburban."

"What's going on?" I asked.

"It seems my husband found out we're here and sent the general to round us up and send us back to Kuwait City." I could tell she was tickled by the attention.

"So?"

"We'd better get going. The general didn't seem to have a sense of humor."

It only took fifteen minutes to collect our things and load the vehicle. I slid behind the wheel and started the engine. Our desert adventure had been cut short, but I felt a small sense of satisfaction that the Senator concurred with my take on the trip—we should not have been there.

As we approached Kuwait City, we saw dozens of burning oil wells in the distance. Everyone wanted to take pictures, and with some encouragement—especially Ken's—I left the highway and headed across the desert. Even though it was late afternoon, we believed we had plenty of time to get back to the city before sunset.

A trail perpendicular to the highway appeared firm enough not to leave us stuck in the sand, so we followed it. At several locations Ken asked me to stop. Everyone piled out of the Suburban and took photographs. We continued, making regular picture stops until the path ended. When we got out of the vehicle for a final photo shoot, we felt the ground shake and heard the distant rumble of the burning wells. Shades of black and gray blotted out any hint of blue above the horizon. Below that dark curtain of sky, I could see countless flames, small because of our distance. From what I had seen on the news and read in papers, however, they were hundreds of feet tall.

With the picture-taking completed, we loaded into the Suburban. Only then did I realize I had no place to turn around. We had driven beyond the end of the tracks and were in sand, clear of tire tracks or foot prints and possibly mined. The sun had started to sink below the desert's edge—it was time to make our way back to the highway. Driving in reverse isn't among my favorite things to do, so I sat on the Suburban's tailgate and shouted commands—left and right—as a braver soul drove us backwards out of the desert.

The day after our return from the refugee camp, we were invited to meet one of the many princes of the Kuwait royal family. Approaching the palace—actually, many palaces, one for each of the royal families—I thought the group of structures looked like a high-security prison. Marble walls approximately twenty-five feet tall surrounded the compound. Within them I could see the tops of numerous buildings. We approached a large, gated opening in the wall and were swarmed by a small army of armed guards, both in uniforms and in plain clothes. After presenting our passports, we were lead to one of the many palaces.

Everything was built of pink-toned marble—exterior walls, interior walls, floors, and ceilings. Heavy, gold, brocade drapes trimmed in fringes of every imaginable style framed the windows. We were shown to a large room—a circle of heavy, gilded chairs in its center—and we waited tentatively for our audience with the prince.

When he arrived, he and an interpreter went around the room and greeted each of us. The prince wore beautifully draped, gold-embroidered robes, and he moved slowly. His handshake was weak, but he made direct eye contact and offered a smile of acknowledgement with each introduction. A man of approximately fifty years, he looked startlingly like Gene Wilder. His complexion was darker, but his protruding eyes, smile, and mannerisms made him a dead ringer for the comedy star. I couldn't help but think of *The Young Frankenstein* and a much scarier palace.

After the individual greetings, he took a seat and began to speak. The interpreter didn't provide a translation, and the prince soon stood and left the room. Our audience was over. While seeing the palace proved interesting, the meeting with Kuwait royalty qualified as a non-event.

It seemed inappropriate to mention the prince's likeness to Gene Wilder, but when we got back to the Suburban, that's what everyone talked about. Cindy seemed unimpressed by the visit to the palace and with the people we'd met. I felt our meet and greet with the royalty had been a nuisance for the prince, so maybe she had the same sense. Yet her attitude suggested annoyance.

From that point forward, Cindy's interest in the trip waned, and she withdrew from group gatherings and tours. She and Ken—often they included me—went on regular photographic outings, but for the most part, the doctors were on their own to schedule surgeries. I felt fortunate to be included in her inner circle and was thrilled by the opportunities to go outside the hospital and take photographs. However, I detected some resentment from Kathy, who was not included in much of the "fun stuff."

At night, when many of the team members gathered to discuss the day's events, Cindy went to her room. She complained of fatigue, but somehow that didn't ring true with me. At times, she was very animated; at others, she appeared drowsy. Given her age, such extremes in energy levels didn't seem natural when her routine remained similar each day.

Because I had learned the streets and felt comfortable driving in Kuwait City, I shuttled the television crews to and from the hospital and the Sheraton Hotel. The Sheraton housed U.S. network television crews that allowed our crews from Tucson and Phoenix to use their editing equipment and transmit stories to our local affiliates. I hoped friends in Phoenix watched the segments about our adventures. If they didn't, I might have trouble convincing them of my apparent new job description.

In addition to my driving duties, I, along with several others, toured hospitals, schools, mosques, and, most memorable to me, a hospital for mentally challenged patients. The cruelty of the Iraqi invaders at that hospital appalled me. Doctors and nurses caring for the patients had been driven away, and the patients were left in their beds to die. The ones we saw—those who had survived—were literally skin and bones. Dressed in loose, white clothing, they lay in metal beds with gray, barred surrounds. The mere sight of them tightened my throat and constricted my breath. To me, they looked like terrified prisoners of war.

Our time in Kuwait passed quickly. When it was time to leave, some of our group seemed unprepared to return to their lives in Arizona. The doctors and nurses had established relationships with local hospital staffs, and our media contingent was possibly covering a once-in-a-lifetime story. Ken had captured images that could never be recreated, and the rest of us—those who provided support—knew we would never again experience a time like the one we had just been privileged to share in Kuwait.

A few people were obviously homesick. Kathy frequently talked about how nice it would be to be home with her husband and children. Barbara, Jeri, and Keri seemed less excited about the return trip. Ken, I think, could have stayed forever. He loved the adventure and appeared thrilled with the pictures he had taken.

Cindy, however, expressed no emotion about returning to Phoenix, her husband, and her children. I realized for the first time that, while on the trip, Cindy didn't talk much about the Senator. In situations where she needed to make an impression, she spoke about him, but otherwise, she didn't talk about her husband or their marriage. I knew from listening to Kathy and Jeri that Cindy and John spent little time together. Cindy voiced her dislike for Washington, and, of course, John's position required that he spend most of his time there. She told me she couldn't imagine raising her kids in D.C. but I couldn't imagine why she would want to raise her kids on her own.

I wondered whether her apparent lack of enthusiasm for the return trip stemmed from spending so much time home alone. She had housekeepers, nannies, groundsmen, but none of these would replace her husband. Children couldn't fill the void left by an absent adult companion. Although I didn't know her well at that point, I'd never heard her mention any friends. On some level, my heart went out to her. Cindy McCain no doubt possessed an overabundance of idle, lonely hours.

We had consumed most of the food and water we brought with us, and we donated the remaining medical supplies to our host hospital. For the return trip, we needed only to be concerned about our personal luggage.

Our flight from Kuwait City on a C130 took us into the Riyadh airport rather than an air force base. Through my counterparts at American Airlines, I had obtained free transportation for our group from there to New York City, so we entered the terminal and checked in like real passengers for our flight back. At JFK Airport in New York, members of AVMT connected to an America West flight to Phoenix. Again, America West provided free transportation for the team. Fortunately, luggage could be checked all of the way through from Riyadh to Phoenix; no one had to handle a bag other than carry-on luggage until reaching home.

Unfortunately, our flight from Riyadh arrived late. With only moments to spare, everyone dashed to the departure gate just in time to catch the connecting flight.

I had made plans to visit friends while in New York, so I didn't travel to Phoenix with the group. However, as I had promised, I escorted everyone from the American Airlines terminal to the Eastern Airlines terminal from which the America West's flights departed. We said our quick good-byes, and I heaved a sigh of relief. My responsibilities to Cindy McCain and the AVMT had been fulfilled. I went back to the Eastern terminal, claimed my bags, and made my way to the taxi queue. Collapsing into the back seat of a cab, I told the driver my destination on West 46th Street and stared out the window. *Finally*, a skyline I recognized.

Despite the comfort of being in a place I knew, an unfamiliar feeling washed over me. In inexplicable ways, I wasn't the same person who had been so often in the Big Apple. Kuwait, Cindy McCain, and the AVMT had changed me. My mind drifted to the team that was now on its way to Phoenix. New friendships—unlikely friendships that otherwise would never have happened—had developed during our time in Kuwait. I can't help but wonder now how many of them still exist.

# Chapter 3

The fun weekend in New York included my birthday celebration and was a welcome respite from the ravaged streets of Kuwait City. I returned to Phoenix refreshed and ready to resume my work at America West.

"How was your trip?" Marty poured a cup of coffee.

"Fantastic." I extended my cup. He filled it.

"Everything went okay?"

"Everything went fine. Our flight into JFK was a little late, but everyone made the connecting flight."

"And?" Marty looked at me over the top of his glasses.

"And what?"

"How was your birthday?"

"Nice. *Very* nice." I smiled.

He nodded and started out of the room. "There's a pile of stuff on your desk. Why don't you go through it and then check in with me."

"You got it."

I went around the corner to my office in an area of the Legal Department that wasn't yet fully occupied. Grace, my coworker, and I were the only people on that side of the building. Whoever arrived first turned on the lights in the common area. They were on.

"Hey, world traveler, how was it?" Grace asked.

She had held several positions at America West, and I wasn't sure all her jobs were promotions. Many of them seemed to have been created specifically for her, and some appeared to bounce her from department to department. I didn't know why, but I didn't care. I liked her and found her easy to work with.

"Grace, I don't think it was your kind of trip, but it was a tremendous experience." Because she loved to take cruises and stay at lavish resorts, I doubted war-ravaged Kuwait would ever be her destination of choice.

"Where'd you stay?" she asked.

"A hospital."

"*What?*"

The look of horror on her face confirmed my suspicion that she would not have found the trip nearly as interesting as I had. I shared some of the details, but beyond the flights and the lodging, she displayed little interest.

My weekend in New York, however, grabbed her attention. Grace could wrap her arms around the Big Apple. She wanted to know all about the Paramount Hotel, the restaurants where I ate, and every detail about where I shopped and what I bought.

"So what was Cindy like?" She raised her eyebrows.

"Really great."

"What did she do? What was her role?"

"She dug in and was right in the middle of everything. There was nothing prima donna-ish about her."

"Really?" The skepticism in her voice made me wonder if I had convinced her.

"Really."

Mid-afternoon, with paperwork still piled high on my desk, my phone rang.

"Hey, Goose. It's Cindy."

She had given me the nickname 'Goose,' apparently short for Gosinski, in Kuwait. I thought it funny, so I didn't protest its sophomoric nature. Because I was the only person she nicknamed, I took it as a compliment of sorts.

"How was your birthday?" she asked.

When I shared the details of my weekend in New York, I was shocked to hear her say she'd not spent much time there. It seemed strange—a person of her stature and wealth had not spent time in New York City? I knew she had gone to university at USC. Perhaps her travels had been confined to the West Coast.

"Goose, I want to thank you for everything you did. You made it a *great* trip."

"Thanks, Cindy. It was fun." Not quite sure how I'd made it a *great* trip, I accepted the gratitude and moved on.

We talked for several minutes and made plans for lunch the following week. She mentioned having some of Ken's pictures to share with me.

I hadn't planned to become friends with Cindy. The trip had been part of my job at America West; nonetheless, I was thrilled she had called and that a friendship seemed to be developing. Our conversation continued with shared stories, observations of the trip, and the people we had traveled with. Before saying goodbye, we confirmed our lunch plans.

The morning of our scheduled lunch, Cindy's assistant called.

"Hey, Kathy, how are you?"

She didn't answer my question. "Tom, Cindy won't be able to have lunch today."

"Okay." I anticipated she'd offer to reschedule. She didn't. After an awkward silence, I repeated, "Okay then…"

"Goodbye," Kathy said.

During our visit to Kuwait, I'd spent little time with Kathy. She kept herself busy at the hospital and appeared comfortable associating with Barbara, Jeri, and Keri. I got the feeling she thought she was being excluded from the excitement, but as Cindy's employee, her relationship and role with Cindy was between them. It had nothing to do with me.

Over the course of the trip, I learned that Kathy was married and had two little girls. She told me her husband had started—or was in the process of starting—a new business, and it was important that she work because he wasn't making much money. They needed her benefits.

My disappointment about not having lunch with Cindy was offset by the time it freed for catching up on my work. I could put the time I'd have spent driving to and from downtown Phoenix and having lunch to good use.

America West's corporate offices sat in downtown Tempe, a suburb southeast of Phoenix. Occupying the first four floors of a five-story building, it also used a campus of buildings across the street for a reservations and training center. The building that housed the offices was part of a mixed-use development of offices, retail space, restaurants, and condominiums. I lived in one of the condominiums, so my commute to work, in heavy pedestrian traffic, took about two minutes. Dashing home for a quick lunch was an option, and I took advantage of the close proximity of my kitchen to fix a quick meal and head back to the office to make the most of my extra time that afternoon.

About a week after the cancelled lunch, I received an invitation to attend an AVMT dinner hosted by the McCains. Prince Al Sabah, Kuwait Ambassador to the United States, would also attend.

Dinner guests were invited to an expansive terraced area behind the McCain's house. The quarried stone terrace, contained two covered structures—one a large, fully-equipped kitchen and well-stocked bar and the other a shelter from the hot Arizona sun. The estate's guest house sat at the north end, and all the structures were finished in the same stucco and tile as the house. Beautifully set round tables covered a large portion of the terrace. Drinks were served at the bar, and a catering team swarmed around the outdoor kitchen.

Attendees included a large congregation of AVMT volunteers that had traveled to Kuwait and their spouses, business owners, or representatives who had donated supplies for the trip, as well as a few people I didn't know or wasn't aware of their association with AVMT. My boss, Marty, and his wife were among the guests. It was great to see many of the people I had met while in Kuwait.

"Goose!" Cindy approached me.

"This is a great party." I looked around at the people who were obviously enjoying themselves.

"You've met my husband, John."

"I have." I gave the Senator's hand a firm shake.

"Goose?" He gave me a curious look.

"A nickname from your wife."

"Ah." He appeared aware of her penchant for bestowing nicknames.

"Tom, I'd like you to meet Ambassador Al Sabah," Cindy said.

I recognized the Ambassador from his many television appearances during the Gulf War. He was a handsome, distinguished man who, I guessed, was educated in the United States because of the quality of his English. I knew from news reports that he was a member of the Kuwait royal family, a prince. I also knew, from a *TIME Magazine* article, that the prince's family had an estimated wealth of $90 billion dollars, with most of its investments in the United States.

"Tom Gosinski." I extended my hand, hating to think he might assume my name was Goose.

"It's very nice to meet you." He took my hand in his. "Were you in Kuwait?"

"I was. I hope to visit it again . . . under different circumstances."

He nodded. "You should."

"Kuwait City is beautiful," I offered.

"Indeed," he replied.

I found Marty and Jo, asked where they intended to sit, and took a seat at their table. The weather was perfect for al fresco dining. The efficient catering staff served food and wine, after which the tables were cleared and coffee and dessert served.

As dinner ended, Cindy went to a portable podium and made some remarks about AVMT's mission, thanked the volunteers and donors who were present, and talked about her hopes for the organization's future. Following her presentation, Senator McCain talked about volunteer work and introduced Ambassador Al Sabah. The Ambassador's comments were short: he thanked AVMT for its work in Kuwait.

Cindy returned to the podium and spoke in a more philosophical way about the characteristics of a volunteer. She lifted a plaque so everyone could see it and read its inscription. Then she said, "In recognition of his hard work and dedication, I'd like to present Tom Gosinski with our Outstanding Volunteer Award."

My breath caught in my throat. Goosebumps broke out on my arms, and I made a mental note not to tell her my nickname was earned that night in a very real way. So many people in the crowd could have been singled out. As a non-medical volunteer, I could hardly believe I had been chosen for this honor.

The Gulf War had taken its toll on many industries, but airlines were among the hardest hit. When fuel prices soared to never-seen-before heights, they hemorrhaged cash and posted record-breaking losses. In the Government and International Affairs department, we focused on Arizona's jet fuel taxes because the escalated prices created a windfall for the state while straining the airlines to the breaking point. America West lobbied for legislation that would create a more equitable tax. We were, at that time, one of the Arizona's largest employers; therefore, we had some clout in the state's capital.

Most of the early-summer months were spent pursuing the new legislation.

A few weeks after the AVMT dinner, I received a call from Kathy.

"Cindy is putting together a small group of people from the Kuwait trip to go to Washington and meet Vice President Quayle. Are you interested?"

"Sure. When is it?"

"We don't have a date yet. I'm trying to find out who might be available."

"Depending on work and the date, yeah, I'd love to go."

"Do you think you might be able to arrange some tickets?"

I'd thought there might be a catch. "I'll see what I can do."

"I'll tell Cindy."

"Thanks." I wondered why I was thanking her. Habit, I guess.

The following week, free tickets arranged through America West in hand, a small group of people representing AVMT's Kuwait trip traveled from Phoenix to Washington D.C. We met the Vice President on the steps of the Old Executive Office Building, a nineteenth-century structure in the Second Empire Style just steps from the White House.

An AVMT nurse presented the Vice President Quayle with a teddy bear that a Kuwaiti girl had given her. The child asked the nurse to see that the bear got to President Bush in recognition of the U.S. liberation of Kuwait from the Iraqi invasion.

Cindy treated the group to lunch in the Senate Dining Room. I don't recall being impressed by the menu, but I couldn't help but be taken by the number of recognizable faces—the most memorable being that of Ted Kennedy.

A picture taken that day, along with other photos from that period of my life, hangs on the wall above my toilet. Its positioning wasn't intentional—I have many pictures hanging in that bathroom—but I'm often amused when I look up and see it.

By mid-summer the airline industry had fallen into catastrophe. Many carriers cancelled plane orders, and some were downsizing their existing fleets. America West closed a few of its money-losing destinations, but, whenever possible, absorbed the employees from those stations into other positions. Although we were bleeding money, management seemed to be adjusting the direction of the company to weather the financial storm.

On June 28, 1991, America West's attempts to turn its luck around ran out. The company entered Chapter 11 bankruptcy, and its future hung in the balance. The announcement of the bankruptcy didn't surprise me because, days before the filing, I'd been asked to collect a check from the company treasurer that was then sent to a Denver law firm that specialized in bankruptcies. Unfortunately, that knowledge precluded me from selling my company stock, which could have been interpreted as insider trading.

Our stock investments, a condition of employment, plummeted along with our confidence in CEO Ed Beauvais. As the company's founder, he had long championed its mission and acted as its visionary, but that vision had grown tarnished. In contrast, Mike Conway, the pragmatic America West President, engendered confidence that made many of us remain positive about the company's ability to survive. Mike didn't sugar-coat the predicament. Instead, he offered brutal, painful remedies that *might* see us out of Chapter 11.

America West filed its bankruptcy papers on a Friday at 5:00 p.m. so that it could prepare for the stock market's reaction on Monday. This gave the company an opportunity to spin its story without reporters including the stock market numbers and reactions from investors. I'd never realized the lengths to which companies go to preserve their public images in such cases.

After work, I walked to my condo and turned on the evening news. The lead story was, of course, America West's bankruptcy. Because of the late filing hour, information was scanty, but the reporter promised to have more on the late edition of the news.

The phone next to my bed jangled. I picked up on the second ring.

"Hey, Tom." It was Cindy.

"What's up?"

"I just heard. How are you?"

"I'm fine…I think things will be okay."

"John seems concerned."

I wondered why he was concerning himself with this. "I really think things will be okay," I repeated.

"I hope so."

We talked for a few more minutes before saying good night. I puttered around the condo for awhile and then decided, since I hadn't been to the gym, it might serve as a distraction. I packed my bag and headed to Beauvais Fitness. Yes, the CEO's son owned the gym. There seemed no escaping that name.

After limited success with releasing my tensions through exercise, I called my friend Todd, and we made plans to go to AZ88 for drinks. AZ88, a trendy Scottsdale lounge and restaurant, served great martinis. My preference was Ketel One vodka with two almond-stuffed olives. Todd would undoubtedly be the remedy for the day's news as his outlook was always bright, light, and fun. It worked, at least for the moment.

\* \* \* \* \*

By Monday morning, all of Phoenix was talking about America West. The news of the Chapter 11 filing filled the front page of every newspaper and was the lead story on every TV station. Television crews set up satellite equipment in front of our headquarters, and reporters pressed everybody to get one-on-one interviews. Security inside the building was tightened; no one without company identification or a scheduled appointment was allowed to board the elevators.

Nobody worked much that day. Most people inside the building felt as anxious about the news as those outside. The day's papers lay strewn across desks to be read and reread. Speculation about the language in the company's press releases dominated almost every conversation.

Would jobs be cut? Would salaries be slashed and benefits eliminated? Would executive heads roll? Would there be a hostile takeover? Everyone wondered. No one knew.

When Cindy and I talked a week later, she asked about my future at America West and whether my job was on the line. Marty had assured me America West would recover from Chapter 11, and my job was secure. Although I wasn't as confident about the company's future as he seemed to be, I had no reason to doubt his prediction. I believe he would have suggested I look for other work had he felt my position was at risk.

During the next months, many people I had worked with from the first year of America West's start up cashed in on the company's buyout options. Structure changes affected several departments, those in charge shuffled management, and the company struggled under a cloud of ongoing doubt.

As a single person with one job, I had not planned for income gaps. I never considered working for another airline but did think about pursuing other career paths. However, I wasn't interested in investing time or money in more education. I'd even flown to Bakersfield, California, to interview for a job with Occidental Petroleum as flight manager for CEO Dr. Ray Irani. That job would have required me to travel the world with Dr. Irani and be on call twenty-four hours a day, 365 days a year. While the position itself offered some attractive perks, living in Bakersfield was not one of them—and that was a requirement.

At some point that summer, Cindy mentioned AVMT needed someone who could set up trips and handle logistics. She'd been impressed with my efforts in making the Kuwait venture work and asked if I could share my expertise on a full-time basis.

Initially, that idea didn't appeal to me. The benefits of working for an airline would be hard to top, and I couldn't imagine giving up my non-revenue flight privileges. Flying to San Diego for dinner, Las Vegas for a night of gambling and shows, and traveling to any of America West's fifty-some destinations for a long weekend or special event had become my way of life. I could visit family in Nebraska any time I desired, and the cost of those visits was minimal. Also, I had formed friendships with many employees at America West, based on our abilities to travel whenever we wanted to wherever we wanted.

My dear friend Carol was my most frequent travel companion. Her husband, a restaurateur, couldn't accompany her, and her parents loved to care for her daughter. This left Carol free to travel whenever she wished. San Diego, Los Angeles, New York City, San Francisco, and London were a few of our favorite destinations. I don't know how many trips we took, but all of them provided fantastic memories. We're still great friends, and I know our friendship was cemented in our far-flung adventures. Those adventures would end if I terminated my America West employment.

Despite the fact that changing jobs meant changing lifestyles, the prospect of working for AVMT grew more appealing as my future with America West continued to be less secure than it had once been. Still, the unknowns concerned me. Cindy and I met on a few occasions to discuss the job's responsibilities, and we agreed my title would be Director of Government and International Affairs. She asked me to meet with Bob Delgado, president of her father's Anheuser-Busch distribution business, to discuss salary.

Hensley & Company offices, located on the west side of Phoenix, sat in an industrial area I had never visited. The building appeared to be a massive warehouse fronted by a smaller office structure. Upon entering the two-story lobby, I marveled at its volume. A huge, glass enclosure in the center of the room housed a bald eagle—whether it was stuffed or a brilliant example of a fake I never learned. In either case, it made me uncomfortable. I know the eagle is part of the Anheuser-Busch logo, but because I see it as an American icon that represents the "land of the free," I found its captive presence in a Plexiglas case to be inappropriate.

On either side of that display, a generously proportioned double stairway curved upward. The furniture, dwarfed by the enormity of the room, seemed as disproportionate as the small reception counter I approached on the left wall.

"My name is Tom Gosinski. I have an appointment with Bob Delgado."

"Please have a seat." The receptionist indicated a grouping of furniture near her desk.

While I waited somewhat impatiently, I continued to study the room's finishes and thumbed through a few of the magazines on the coffee table.

"Tom?" I heard a voice from the top of the stairway.

"Yes."

I stood, started up the stairs, and extended my hand to the man standing one step above me. The stairs might have been useful if they were intended to intimidate visitors or provide an opportunity for employees to exercise, but I thought them overly grandiose.

"Bob Delgado. Please call me Bob."

I had anticipated someone older, but he appeared to be forty-ish. Expensive clothes and nice, well-polished shoes accentuated his Italian good looks, dark hair, great tan, and athletic build.

"Let's go to my office." He bounded up the remaining stairs.

Because he was taller than my five feet eight inches, I hustled to keep up with him. Following him into an enormous office, I noted the generous seating—a table for four, a large desk with matching credenza, guest chairs, and a variety of smaller cabinets and accessory pieces. Even with all that furniture, he had abundant room for more. We sat at the table.

"Cindy tells me you're going to work for AVMT."

"I'm not sure. We've been discussing it."

"How are things at America West?"

"Improving, I think. As Ed Beauvais says, 'You have to slow a ship down before you can turn it around.'"

"We're all hoping things get better."

I wondered where Hensley & Company ranked in the list of America West's creditors. I assumed that much of the beer served on its flights was provided by Hensley.

"What do you see as your function at AVMT?" Bob asked.

I explained that I could offer a variety of management skills and, specifically, bring my knowledge of the airline industry to the organization. I knew he was aware of the free tickets I'd obtained for AVMT's trips to Kuwait and Washington D.C., so I didn't remind him about that.

Bob seemed nice, as genuine as he was easy to talk to. Our meeting wasn't long. By its end, we had agreed on a salary, and he explained my benefits would be provided through

Hensley & Company. I didn't commit to his offer on the spot, but I left the meeting knowing I had options.

I contemplated AVMT's offer for a few days. I really liked my job at America West, and I thought the world of my boss, Marty. On the other hand, working for Cindy seemed a sound financial decision, and traveling with AVMT would be exciting if the trip to Kuwait had been any indication. I had been to many of the world's glamorous destinations; the opportunity to explore its underbelly intrigued me.

When I had decided my direction, I drafted a resignation letter. Marty's secretary, Sarah, typed my letters. As she read through the draft, she gave me an inquisitive look.

"Are you sure?" she asked.

"I think I am."

"Does Marty know? What do you plan to do?"

"I'll tell you after I've talked to Marty."

"We're going to miss you."

"Thanks."

Sarah tucked the letter in the top drawer of her desk when a secretary from another department walked in. She smiled at me. "I'll let you know when I'm done with your letter."

Marty always got to work early, so the next morning, before anyone else had arrived, I went to his office and presented my resignation. He read it and, without saying anything, looked over the top of his glasses at me and wagged his head from side to side.

"What's this?"

"It's my resignation."

"I know that. What's it about?"

"I'm going to go to work for Cindy McCain at AVMT. Director of Government and International Affairs."

"Are you sure that's what you want to do?"

I didn't want to tell Marty my concerns about the viability of America West in general or, more specifically, middle-management jobs. I felt sure he'd heard all those stories before, and I didn't want to add to his burden or make him feel as though he had to offer me more encouraging words.

"I'm sure. It sounds like an exciting job, and there's bound to be some great travel," I said.

"I'll hate to see you leave."

I swallowed hard to keep from tearing up. Few people I've ever met were as decent or as thoughtful as Marty. He'd gone out of his way to be kind to me, and I considered him a true mentor.

"How about I keep this letter in my desk and put you on sabbatical for a few months? If you want to come back . . . your job will still be here."

I'll never forget the generosity of Marty's offer. Looking back now, I realize it seemed strange and somewhat ominous. But at the time I couldn't imagine why he thought I might want to return.

# Chapter 4

My transition from America West Airlines to the American Voluntary Medical Team went seamlessly. I left the airline on a Friday and started my new job on Monday.

AVMT's offices were situated in a new, small building in downtown Phoenix. Adjacent to it, a two-story structure provided parking. Our four-office suite on the first floor included a general use space and reception area.

Jeri Johnson greeted me as I opened the door to the suite. She served as the receptionist. Kathy's job, harder to define, included working as a coordinator for AVMT and also as Cindy's secretary at Hensley & Company. Both job descriptions lacked definition.

"Good morning, Tom. Welcome to AVMT." Jeri's cheery greeting made me feel right at home. I'd had limited exposure to her in Kuwait, but I'd enjoyed her company and her attitude the few times we were together. She displayed the confidence and sophistication one acquires with age and experience.

"Hey, Tom." I recognized Kathy's voice but I couldn't see her. "You can use this office."

"Where are you?" I still didn't see her.

"I'm in your new office. Come on in." I saw the light come on and realized Kathy was in an office on the south side of the space.

I entered the door to my new space. The windows faced south, so I was happy with its exposure to daylight.

The tasteful furniture—desk, small credenza, and assorted chairs—satisfied my desire for an aesthetically pleasing workspace.

"Would you like some coffee?" Jeri stood in the doorway, two cups of steaming brew in her hands.

"I'd love some."

She brought it to my desk and sat down in one of the guest chairs. I asked about Barbara, the other AVMT employee who had traveled to Kuwait, and Jeri told me Cindy had terminated her the previous week. I wondered if I had replaced her. This was the only time Barbara's name was mentioned after I began my job there.

I didn't receive a job description or a list of responsibilities, so I spent the first few days trying to figure out what to do. Kathy seemed too busy to explain anything. Jeri, on the other hand, took the time to help me settle in. I didn't hear from Cindy during my first few days; however, I was told she was busy with other things at the house.

Jeri showed me press clippings from AVMT's trips prior to Kuwait and albums of photographs. She even offered brief, insightful biographies of various volunteers captured in some of the pictures. As a retired dancer and dance teacher, she shared fascinating stories about her youth. I thoroughly enjoyed her company.

After a few days of reading through files and learning as much as I could about AVMT, I finally heard from Cindy.

"Hey, Goose. Are you getting settled?"

"I am." Getting settled had only taken a few hours, but I didn't want to expound upon my idle time at AVMT.

"Has Kathy told you about the fundraising letter we've been working on and the trip to Bangladesh?"

"No, she hasn't."

The communication between Kathy and me had been almost nonexistent. She'd taken time to let me know she had no idea what I was supposed to do, but she never attempted to share the daily goings-on of the office. Jeri and I had gone through a variety of files, and it was obvious from looking at them that Kathy was involved with every aspect of AVMT. I'd have thought she would be happy to have some help.

Cindy interrupted my disconcerting reverie. "I've been working on some plans for fundraising with a consultant from D.C. I'd like you to get up to speed on it because I want you involved. Also, I'd like to go to Bangladesh next month."

"I'll ask Kathy for the fundraising stuff. What's been done on the Bangladesh trip?"

"I don't know what Kathy's done. I'll give her a call." Cindy hung up.

A few minutes later, Kathy appeared at my door. "Cindy said you need this." She placed a file marked "Fundraising" on my desk.

"What about the Bangladesh file?"

"Bangladesh file?"

"Cindy mentioned she wants to go to Bangladesh next month."

"Oh, yeah. I've not done anything about that. You know, I also have to do Cindy's Hensley stuff, too."

"I know. Tell me what we need for the Bangladesh trip, and I can help you." Beginning to understand Kathy's frustration, I lifted the Fundraising file. "So what about this one?"

"I've been working on it for a month. Cindy said she wants you to work on it now." She walked away.

The fundraising folder consisted of several sample mass-mailers and a rough draft of an AVMT letter. Portions of the four-page document were blank—apparently spaces for photographs. In reading through it, I was taken by the number of grammatical and typing errors; but because it was a rough draft, I overlooked them and decided the project could wait until after the Bangladesh trip had been organized.

With the Bangladesh trip just six weeks away, we had a lot of work to do. I asked Jeri to compile a list of volunteers who might want to travel with us and suggested that Kathy help. Cindy hadn't mentioned what the focus of the trip would be, so I made a prioritized list of generic tasks to be accomplished. Transportation, lodging, and supplies topped my list. It didn't take long to secure free airline tickets and cargo transportation. Cindy decided we'd visit several small clinics, so our need to transport medical equipment was minimal. We could use the clinics' equipment.

One day, while preparing for the trip, I received a call from Cindy. She asked me to meet her at the Hensley & Company building in west Phoenix. When I arrived, she was practically bubbling over with excitement.

"Goose, you have to see these."

We had gone up to a large, caged, storage room on the second floor of the building. She walked over to two huge, red, metal cases on casters.

"What are they?" I asked.

"I had them custom-made to carry our supplies." She unlatched an upright chest that stood approximately five feet tall and was three feet by three feet in depth and width. The front of the chest opened much like an old travel steamer and revealed a bank of drawers in varying sizes. All the flat surfaces were red; the edges and corners were bracketed in chrome fittings.

"Wow. That's something." I felt like I was offering appropriate appreciation for an ugly Christmas gift.

"Yes. We'll be able to transport everything in these cases." She grinned like a child with a new toy.

"And what about this one?" I went to the second case, which was about the size of a refrigerator lying on its side and finished in the same red and chrome.

"This one opens into a portable bed." After several minutes of opening latches, tugging at a telescoping table surface, and unfolding collapsible legs, she succeeded in creating a makeshift bed. "Won't this be fantastic?"

"Uh . . . yes." I couldn't imagine either case being of use. Their weight alone would make that unmanageable with anything less than a forklift.

Later, it took only a few questions to Kathy to discover neither she nor Cindy had consulted with anybody before ordering the cases. Thousands of dollars had no doubt been wasted because their size excluded them from being carried by any airline flying in and out of Phoenix—neither of them would fit through the cargo doors of a 737 or 757. I called Cindy and told her the bad news as gently as I could. She seemed to accept it but was determined to take the smaller case to Bangladesh. We decided to truck it to LAX, where it could be loaded on a 747. I shook my head at what I considered to be a huge waste of resources and a horribly inefficient manner of transporting supplies. Apparently, Cindy really did need my help and my expertise; I settled more comfortably into my new responsibilities.

It didn't take long to put together the Bangladesh trip, and I began to sense a positive shift in Kathy's attitude toward my contributions to AVMT. I used my contacts to obtain free transportation and reduced lodging rates in Bangladesh. We would fly America West to LAX and then transfer to Thai Airways. The trip would be long: Phoenix to Los Angeles, then Tokyo, Bangkok, and, finally, Dhaka.

A week later, Cindy and I met with the fundraising consultants and reviewed the AVMT letter's format, photographs that might be used, and need for a mailing list. The consultants suggested several sources for buying mailing lists and explained the benefits. The importance of demographics couldn't be overemphasized because the success of the mass mailing depended upon the number of responses. Elderly people with conservative values who had responded to similar mailings became the target audience.

Vital considerations included the production of the letter, its printing, mailing list costs, and postage. Because the rate of return from mass mailings is minimal, the ability of the consultants to target a responsive audience was key. I stated my concerns about the cost of the mailing, but Cindy insisted it would be effective.

The laborious preparation and proofing of the letter evolved into an air of excitement when it finally went to press. We planned for the mailer to be distributed as soon as we returned from Bangladesh. The response envelopes were addressed to AVMT's office so we'd be able to immediately measure its effectiveness. It was with an air of dual anticipation, then, that we set out on our journey.

## Chapter 5

Approximately twenty people traveled to Bangladesh, a perfect number for this limited trip. Mark Salter from Senator McCain's Washington, D.C., office secured Visas and also helped establish the itinerary. We planned to visit the International Center for Diarrheal Diseases Research and the Sister of Charity Orphanage established by Mother Teresa. The long flight culminated in our almost surreal arrival at the Dhaka airport.

As the aircraft taxied to the terminal, we saw thousands of people lining the fences around the perimeter of the airport. At first, we thought the crowds must be there to witness something extraordinary, but a flight attendant informed us that people stood outside the airport fences every day to watch planes take off and land. This disturbing scene introduced the impoverished nation of Bangladesh.

Once inside the terminal, we went through customs. Cindy traveled with a diplomatic passport, and I assumed that expedited our processing. After claiming our checked luggage, we were escorted to cars at curbside. Crowds massed around the exit. Two rows of armed soldiers formed a corridor for us to reach our waiting transportation.

Dhaka roads overflowed with old vehicles, overloaded buses, and all forms of bicycles, pedaled rickshaws, and carts. Women balanced large, clay pots and baskets on the tops of their heads. Men and children herded all types of farm animals on the roads' shoulders.

The congestion continued all the way to the walled hotel compound. Once we entered the driveway, the crowds disappeared, kept at bay at the edge of the hotel's property. Given what we had already seen, we were pleased by the presence of a relatively new, modernly equipped Sheraton hotel in the center of Dhaka. The lobby, although somewhat dated, was nicely furnished and clean. After checking in, we retreated to our rooms to unpack, wash up, and relax.

While in Bangladesh, I roomed with John "Max" Johnson, a soft-spoken cardiologist from Phoenix. I'd become acquainted with him during AVMT's trip to Kuwait, but because of the size of that group, our interaction had been limited. Cindy liked Max and had asked him to serve as AVMT's Medical Director. Although his position was voluntary, all his expenses were covered. People appeared to view him as an authority figure—perhaps because of his quiet confidence—and everyone seemed to be charmed by his Southern manners. He spoke in a controlled, slow cadence with an ever-so-slight stammer.

"Tom, which bed do you want?" he asked.

"I don't care."

"Then I'll take the one closest to the bathroom. I get up during the night." He tossed his bag on his claimed bed.

We both unpacked and organized our things in the dresser drawers. When we had finished, I looked up to see him stifle a yawn. Fatigue lined his face. It had been an exhausting trip, and he wasn't a young man.

"Max, why don't you take a short nap? We don't need to be downstairs for an hour."

"I think I will." He stretched out on his bed, crossed his legs at the ankle, and placed his hands on his stomach. In a few minutes he snored softly.

The team met in the hotel's restaurant and decided to eat from the buffet rather than order from the menu. I took

Pepto Bismol tablets prophylactically, and we chose cooked and baked items and fruits that could be peeled. We were careful not to drink sodas with ice or things that might have been rinsed in local water. Bangladesh's biggest killer was common diarrhea. The water supply wasn't safe.

With hours of sunlight remaining after dinner, we opted to explore nearby neighborhoods. Immediately outside the hotel's walls, we confronted more realities of third world life. The streets teemed with small, old vehicles and rickshaws. A deafening cacophony of horns and thumb chimes filled the air. The rickshaws were equipped with the same type of thumb chimes we all had on our childhood bikes.

A few blocks from the hotel, we encountered a sea of cardboard and corrugated metal huts. Actually, they didn't even qualify as huts, but seemed more like houses of cards, each attached to the next. If one collapsed, likely the entire group would collapse.

The rows of houses backed onto alley-like areas with tiny packed-dirt backyards that sloped slightly toward the center. It only took moments to realize the area sloped so that fluids—dish water, bath water, human waste, and so forth—that emanated from underneath the hut walls would run into the shallow, slow-moving stream separating the rows of shacks. Barefoot children and their mangy-looking pets congregated and played along the sewage-ways.

Ken and his camera took full advantage of the scene. His lenses undoubtedly feasted on the juxtaposition of materials, the squalor, and the native dress. I envied his ability to remove himself from the situation and be absorbed by the beauty of Bangladesh's color and texture.

The next morning, after a breakfast of bread and hot tea, we departed for the orphanage. Located on Islampur Road in Old Dhaka—an ancient part of the city composed of decaying stucco buildings and accessed by narrow, cobbled streets—its front exterior sat on the edge of the road, as did the surrounding structures' facades. Many of the building fronts displayed scars from car bumpers because it was impossible to pass an oncoming car or cart without coming to a complete stop so the other vehicle could inch by.

From the outside, the orphanage appeared like all the other buildings facing the street, its facade without distinguishable features. The only way to find our destination was to watch the hand-painted street numbers on the door openings. When we finally arrived, we unfolded ourselves from the small, packed cars and huddled at the door so we could enter as a group.

Inside the building, nuns in long, white, loose robes with the traditional blue and white head scarves hustled children in every direction. Cleaning ladies swept the floors, and older children played games with younger children. After introductions and explanations hampered by language barriers, the nun who greeted us went to get our host. Much to our delight, a small, childlike woman appeared. Obviously, the sister in charge, she couldn't have been taller than four feet, ten inches. Although her vestments covered a tiny frame, her eyes communicated the confidence of a much larger person.

The sister gave us a well-rehearsed tour of the building. She might have conducted the tour before, but her engaging presentation could not have been fresher or more sincere. The building's large rooms and wide hallways suggested it had been a school in another life. Most of the downstairs rooms appeared to be administrative offices and classrooms. At the center of the building, a wide, generously proportioned staircase led to more large rooms on the second floor, many of which held numerous beds and cribs. Sheets of fabric hanging from wires stretched from wall to wall partitioned the large space into a series of smaller rooms.

One room held the orphanage's infants, its newest arrivals. The babies looked well-fed and clean. Nuns of all ages pampered the little ones, who were wrapped in all colors of infant wear and blankets. Within minutes, we each held a baby in our arms, cooing and comparing our bundles of joy. All of them looked at us out of dark, beautiful eyes, and most had dark tufts of hair atop their heads.

A beautiful little girl with black, piercing eyes and silky, dark skin grabbed our attention. It wasn't until the sister moved a piece of soft, pastel fabric that covered the baby's lower face that we noticed her severe harelip. The precious little girl's smile was broken by the gap that split her upper lip. The sister then showed us that a portion of the roof of her mouth opened to the nasal cavity in a large cleft palate. Regardless, the little girl did what she could to turn up the corners of her mouth and give us a happy smile. I didn't want to think about the fact that, without medical intervention, she would too soon have little to smile about.

After leaving the orphanage, we returned to the hotel, where the doctors and nurses prepared medical kits for our visit to the International Center for Diarrheal Diseases Research, ICDDR. The large, red chest that had accompanied us to Bangladesh was secured in Cindy's room, so the medical personnel met there to access their supplies. Unsure what they would encounter, they equipped themselves with an array of thermometers, stethoscopes, gauzes, and wraps. The doctors were provisioned with controlled pharmaceutical drugs and pain pills. It wasn't until the distribution of medical supplies that I learned the controlled drugs hadn't traveled to Bangladesh in the chest, but instead had been transported in Cindy's carryon bag.

I thought it odd that Cindy carried the controlled drugs and wondered whether it was appropriate because her diplomatic passport exempted her carryon bags from being searched. However, she made it seem standard procedure, so I didn't question it. Also, I didn't understand why we traveled with that cumbersome trunk if, in fact, it wasn't used to

transport the drugs. We certainly didn't need all those drawers and bins designed to carry bottles of drugs that were, in
fact, in Cindy's bags.

The relative newness of the single-story, brick and stucco
ICDDR structure contrasted sharply with many of Dhaka's
buildings. By the time we arrived, hundreds of people already
waited in line to get in. Fortunately, a guard noticed our arrival and ushered us into a room the size of a gymnasium.
Naugahyde-covered examination tables of waist height, set
like rows of desks in a huge classroom, occupied the bulk
of the space. Naturally lit by banks of open windows on the
walls to the left and right, the room benefited from the cross-
ventilation that carried out the foul odors that otherwise
would have permeated the air.

An ICDDR doctor joined our group and explained the
center's function. As we walked through the rows of beds, he
told us that the high rate of diarrhea and diarrhea-related diseases taxed their resources, but the ICDDR did what it could
to remedy the epidemic. Having seen the cardboard city, we
understood the extent of the problem.

Most of the patients suffered from extreme dehydration.
The center rehydrated as many as possible, providing appropriate medication to deter additional disease if necessary. As
we toured the facility, we learned the function of the examination tables.

In the center of each, a Naugahyde-lined hole created a
chute of sorts to a bucket that sat on the floor below. Patients
on the tables, their butts over the holes, received intravascu-
lar fluid to offset the dehydration. When they retained more
fluid than they lost—the IV volume compared to the bucket
volume—they were released. The bed was then washed and
prepared for the next patient. I couldn't help but wonder
about sending patients back into the same filthy environment
from which they had come. With such a revolving-door situation, how could the problem ever be resolved?

The most heartbreaking patients were the infants. Because of the fragility of the babies' arm veins, many of them endured IVs piercing the skin of their scalps. The small, blue veins that crossed their heads carried the nutrients necessary to keep them living.

By the end of our tour, several doctors and nurses from AVMT's ranks had volunteered to spend several days at the ICDDR, assisting in the never-ending rehydrating of the population that had no hope other than to return when the diarrhea again threatened their lives.

That evening after dinner, a small group of us took a tour of the city. Just outside the hotel's walls, we flagged down a few rickshaws and started our journey of the city. Dhaka, like many of its counterparts, consisted of a series of neighborhoods, each with its own demographic. I shared a rickshaw with Ken and Cindy, so there was never a lack of commentary regarding our surroundings.

Some thirty minutes into our outing, it started to rain—a torrential downpour. Soon, the water had risen to the hub of the rickshaw's bicycle-size front tire and neared the height of the pedal-powered transport's footrest. The deluge stalled traffic, and we found our rickshaw and those of our AVMT comrades consumed by a monumental traffic jam. By then, the water flowed over the top of the footrest. To avoid the sewage that flowed along with the floodwater, we squatted on our seat, laughing hysterically as blaring bus horns and rickshaw thumb chimes created a dissonant chorus we would never have heard at home.

The following morning, a small group of AVMT volunteers departed for the remote cities of Rangpur and Rajshahi, while others stayed in Dhaka to continue their work at the ICDDR. Cindy busied herself with the task of arranging for two babies from the orphanage to travel to the United States for needed medical treatment—the infant with the cleft palate and one with a heart defect. I overheard her make several calls to prepare for the arrival of both babies in Phoenix.

She had taken a particular liking to the baby with the cleft palate, and she contacted a member of John's Phoenix staff, Wes, to see if he and his wife would be interested in adopting the second baby. I thought it odd for her to be planning to adopt the little girl and seeking parents for the other child. My understanding was that the babies could be taken from Bangladesh only for medical care. They were to be returned once they had received that care.

"Can you believe it? These babies will have such wonderful lives." Cindy's ecstatic smile conveyed her joy.

"They're going to receive great care." I agreed.

"Wes and Pam are so excited."

"I'm sure they are." I still had misgivings about removing them from their homeland, particularly since that seemed contrary to the rules. "Did John seem excited by the news?" I asked.

"He didn't say much."

"She's gonna need lots of care." I said.

"I can give it to her." Cindy nodded with conviction.

The fact that John didn't care if Cindy brought home a baby would have seemed weird if they had been a regular family. Given that they were the McCains, however, it seemed reasonable. I'd realized early on that her life was separate from her husband's. Certainly, their paths crossed, and publicly they presented themselves as a couple. But in reality, it didn't seem to matter what she did when he wasn't around, which was most of the time.

Prior to our departure from Bangladesh, we had to obtain passports and visas for the babies. Generally, the processing of such paperwork took considerable time. However, we were leaving soon, so the process had to be expedited. Cindy complained about the slowness of Bangladesh officials, but had they known she had no intention of returning the babies, I doubt they would have issued the documents at all.

Our last night in Bangladesh, the babies slept in Cindy's room—in dresser drawers lined with blankets. AVMT members were in and out of the room and, if they were lucky, took a turn at feeding, bouncing, and burping.

Max and I occupied the next room, and as members visited Cindy, they also visited us. Even though everyone was anxious to go home, I sensed varying degrees of nostalgia among them. The overwhelming needs of the destitute people no doubt tugged at their hearts as it did mine and contributed to the melancholy over our departure.

Max and I talked about AVMT's future and his role in the organization. In semi-retirement, he saw AVMT as a unique way of transitioning from his cardiology career to doing other things. Excited by the prospects of his role, he seemed equally thrilled by the opportunity to travel. He even hoped to include his wife, Jeannette, on trips she would find interesting.

"Tom, where do you see yourself in ten years?" he asked.

"I don't know. AVMT seems like a worthwhile organization, but I'm not sure I want to do this forever. Politics has some allure—the background stuff, not being a politician. I don't think I'd be good at playing that game."

"You need to be careful." Max was changing the topic.

"Of what?"

"Appearances. You don't want to appear to be too close to Cindy."

I didn't reply. I knew what Max was inferring. My relationship with Cindy wasn't conventional, but it also wasn't suspicious. I know Max didn't understand the nature of our relationship, and I wasn't about to explain it to him. Discomfort settled over me.

\* \* \* \* \*

The next morning everyone came to breakfast early and seemed anxious to start the trip home. Cindy had told me she'd made arrangements with the Hensley & Company pilot to meet her at LAX and transport her, the babies, and one of the nurses back to Phoenix; and I was present when she'd talked to Pam and Wes about their "delivery." She also told John to be at the airport to greet their new daughter. Of course, she'd asked that the press be notified so they could document the arrival of the babies.

Her decision to fly to Phoenix ahead of the rest of the members of the AVMT mission and to have journalists and photographers awaiting her arrival, in my opinion, defies reason, but that didn't really matter. Both of those little girls from Bangladesh who had had little hope for a future would be given every benefit the world can offer.

## Chapter 6

Within a few days of our return from Bangladesh, Cindy named the little girl with the cleft palate Bridget. She asked me to accompany the two of them to many of the baby's medical appointments, possibly because of John's absence. This allowed her to devote her full attention to the baby while I negotiated our way through traffic. It also allowed me to feel somehow invested in Bridget's welfare.

I recall the first of her many surgeries. As with the leg amputation I'd observed in Kuwait, I could look at Bridget's small, fragile face with a detachment I didn't know I possessed. Because of the swelling around her mouth, the skin of her face and lips was drawn taut and appeared glossy, like a balloon inflated to almost bursting. I could not help but wonder what she was thinking and tried to interpret the thoughts she seemed to be offering from the deep, rich black of her questioning eyes. My own thoughts kept returning to the orphanage where we'd found her, and I shuddered when I considered what her life might have been had Cindy not brought her to Phoenix. Unquestionably, Cindy's care for Bridget was one of the most generous acts of kindness I'd ever witnessed.

Prior to our trip to Bangladesh, Cindy called me countless times a day—she called everyone at AVMT several times a day—but after the trip, she started to call me evenings at home. Sometimes the calls were work related; more often, they simply related something funny her kids had said or done. Meghan was, I believe, in kindergarten. Preschoolers Jack and Jimmy would then have been an age that made almost everything they did or said seem amusing.

One night, at about eleven o'clock, Cindy called. "That bitch is on T.V."

"What? Who?" I had no idea what she was talking about.

"Madonna is on Letterman."

Cindy knew I was a fan of Madonna, so she'd called to make sure I didn't miss her appearance on Letterman. At the time it seemed odd because I made it a rule not to call people after ten at night. However, I also thought it was funny, so I didn't give it much thought. Cindy and I were becoming friends outside the workplace; like my other friends, she knew I seldom got to bed before midnight.

Finally, the fundraising letter we'd spent weeks working on was ready for distribution. We eagerly awaited the huge bags of mail containing the anticipated influx of donations. Instead, a smattering of envelopes trickled in with many of the responses marked "DECEASED."

The mass mailing had been a financial disaster, as well as an embarrassment. We lost thousands of dollars, but more upsetting to me was the purchase of outdated mailing lists that included a significantly larger than expected number of names and addresses of deceased individuals. What must their grieving family members have thought about AVMT's pitches for money from their dead loved ones?

Seemingly unperturbed by the ineffectiveness of the fundraising letters, Cindy commented that the mailing had been a good way for AVMT to spread its name. Her lack of concern puzzled me. Was it because she'd contracted the firm that provided the names and didn't want to take responsibility for the outcome? Or was the loss of a few thousand dollars no big deal to her? Regardless, I seemed to be the only person who felt alarmed.

A few months into my tenure at AVMT, Cindy hired another new employee, Tracy, a former intern from Senator McCain's Phoenix office and a new graduate of Arizona State University. Tracy was young, blonde, and attractive. Cindy hired her to handle AVMT's press relations. I couldn't imagine that the job justified a full-time position, but I assumed Cindy had a plan. I liked Tracy. She brought youthful vigor and enthusiasm to our staff. Although her job description was vague, I knew she'd be fun to have around. We'd muddle our way through AVMT together.

The only person who truly had a defined job description was Jeri: receptionist. She more than anyone else, I believed, understood the lack of organization within AVMT.

Kathy's situation, on the other hand, seemed more precarious. Her responsibilities included duties at AVMT *and* Hensley & Company, either of which could constitute a full-time job. She had helped Cindy with AVMT since its inception and probably had more knowledge of its structure than anyone. She knew the doctors and nurses who'd worked with the organization and had access to all its records. Added staff redefined Kathy's job, but she seemed reluctant to let go of her responsibilities as Cindy redistributed the workload. For example, Cindy assigned many of the travel opportunities to Tracy and me, leaving Kathy to handle clerical tasks of correspondence, filing, and inventory. Of course, she still had her responsibilities as Cindy's personal secretary, but at times I got the feeling she resented us, perhaps because we received the more interesting assignments.

Cindy envisioned AVMT in constant motion, its back-to-back trips reaching all corners of the globe to bring relief and care in areas devastated by natural disasters and war. By virtue of its nature, AVMT generated more excitement than did Kathy's secretarial duties at Hensley & Company. Unfortunately for Kathy, Cindy's grander plans for AVMT didn't appear to include her. Kathy had reason to be upset—she had been an integral part of AVMT's birth and growth.

When I met Kathy, she had been Cindy's employee for several years. I don't know how she came to work for Cindy, but her lack of sophistication made her an odd choice in my mind. She presented herself as an executive secretary, but something was always "off" about her appearance. Her frumpy clothes, outdated hairstyle, and make-up choices indicated a 1970s Midwest upbringing that still held her captive. There's nothing wrong with the 70s or the Midwest, and I know one should not judge a person solely by appearance. However, I'd worked with numerous professional secretaries—it was hard to not make distinctions. She also struggled with basic writing skills required to compose a simple business letter, and her lack of self-confidence was obvious to nearly everyone.

Few people would have wanted Kathy's job. As executive secretary, she managed Cindy's schedule, which consisted of many public appearances as a corporate officer at Hensley and Company and as a Senator's wife. That job also included ensuring that Cindy stuck to her schedule. However, Cindy seemed to cancel as many appointments as she kept, and Kathy had to make her excuses and take a blistering from disappointed—sometimes angry—event organizers who had publicly promoted Cindy's attendance. Kathy took her work personally and often was reduced to tears. She repeatedly expressed her concern that those cancellations and no-show calls put her personal credibility in doubt.

As Kathy's job evolved, Cindy didn't provide her with explanations. Sometimes, Jeri, Tracy, or I had to inform her about changes or tell her she was or wasn't traveling with AVMT. I'd never witnessed such dysfunction in a work environment, and the way many situations were handled seemed very unfair to Kathy, whose loyalty to Cindy appeared above reproach. Cindy obviously had the upper hand, but I was appalled at her lack of compassion for Kathy's feelings.

## Chapter 7

I thought Hanoi would be different. I anticipated bumper-to-bumper traffic, derelict buildings, and overgrown flora, but discovered a city filled with untold numbers of people scurrying around on bikes, French-influenced architecture, and manicured landscapes.

On our first morning in Hanoi, my new opinion was reinforced by an unbelievable sight. Around six o'clock, I woke to the sound of a low, waling horn.

"What's that?" I asked.

"I don't know," Ken replied.

When I looked out the window, people on the streets were doing tai chi—an exercise of slow, fluid motions—in almost perfect synchronization.

"That's amazing." I couldn't take my eyes off the strangely beautiful sight. The streets had been transformed into an open fitness center, and everyone seemed to be a member. Men, women, and children of all ages appeared to have come alive with the common objective of keeping their nation fit. As I scanned the open space outside the dorm-like building where we were housed, I saw no one obese. Rather, the population was thin, trim, and energetic. I found myself mystified at the sight.

AVMT's trip to Vietnam was different for two reasons: First, we were visiting the country where John McCain had been held prisoner during the Vietnam conflict. Second, we went with the goal of doing a greater amount of surgical work.

As I understood, AVMT was one of the few groups—with the exception of the French—that had brought Western medicine to the country since the end of the conflict in 1975.

I'd had observed a number of surgeries in Kuwait—the leg amputation being the most memorable—so when I had a chance to watch surgeries in Hanoi, I was excited by the prospect. We weren't asked to scrub or wear surgical gowns, but were required to don a hair cap and a pair of disposable shoe covers. Those directly involved in the surgeries practiced sterile procedures, but because we were farther back in the room, those stringent requirements didn't apply to us.

The operating room appeared clean, but I was shocked by the absence of air conditioning. Large, open windows lined one wall, and big fans, placed in the windows, circulated the air. Because the surgery I was observing required a portion of the skull to be removed, the female patient was seated upright in a chair that had been rigged with painted wooden slats to support the length of her arms. Both weathered pieces of wood looked as though they needed a good coat of paint.

A large group of Vietnamese doctors congregated in the room to watch AVMT's team perform the procedure. I don't recall the specific type of surgery, but I do remember that everyone involved expressed concern about the complexity of the case. Volker Sonntag, a neurosurgeon from the Barrow Neurological Institute, had joined us on this trip, and the Vietnamese doctors were eager to watch him operate. In spite of the heat and the crowded quarters, the surgery went smoothly.

While in Hanoi, the team went to see a statue at Truc Bach Lake that commemorated the location where the Vietnamese had shot down the aircraft piloted by John McCain. The size of the lake, which was located in a park in central Hanoi that was roughly equivalent to New York City's Central Park, could not be estimated from our vantage point. The fact that we were not told how far from shore John was at the time of his capture added to our inability to visualize the scene. The stone statue, a modern interpretation of the event, depicted McCain as a United States Air Force pilot—USAF was carved in the stone. He was, however, a Navy pilot—the son of Admiral John S. McCain, Jr., which made his capture front-page news in North Vietnam. On another of our outings through the city, our guide pointed to a structure and told us it was the "Hanoi Hilton," the building where POWs were held during the conflict.

Cindy had been noticeably shaken by the sight of the monument and now the "Hanoi Hilton." Ken took many pictures to document the landmarks that brought harsh reality to the stories of her husband's experiences as a POW, but the beauty of the park seemed a stark contrast to the circumstances of the monument. I thought about all the other American soldiers who had suffered at the hands of their captors. They weren't as big a "catch" as John McCain and didn't rate a memorial.

Our group's mood, sobered by the visit to the monument, returned to a more spirited level when we returned to the government guest house.

It's hard to imagine how the McCains' lives might have differed had John McCain not been shot down over Hanoi. Would he have continued his military service and ascended to the heights of his father's and grandfather's careers? Would he and Cindy Hensley have met while both were in Hawaii? Would he have divorced his first wife to marry the beer baron's daughter? Would he have pursued the political career that catapulted him into national prominence because of his war-hero background? We'll never know.

I recalled a conversation with my friend Ted shortly before I left America West.

"You really think you want to work for a McCain?" Ted asked.

"Yeah. Why not?"

"You know he wouldn't even be a Senator if he'd been a better pilot."

"You're nuts." I chuckled because Ted always had a funny way of stating what everyone else was thinking but didn't dare say. Of course, like all good humor, it contained an element of truth and caused me to pause and consider my future.

"I'll be fine." I don't know whether I was trying to convince Ted or myself.

One of my memories of our trip to Vietnam was a lunch hosted by a group of local doctors. We drove to a small restaurant that looked like a remodeled, flat-roofed gas station. After making our way through a small dining room, an even smaller kitchen that held a galvanized tank filled with fish, and up a small set of stairs to the top of the building that was covered by a thatched roof, we drank strong beer and peered at a menu that none of us understood. Despite the language barrier, we finally communicated that the doctors should order for us and we could eat the meal family style.

As platters of fried food smelling of old cooking oil arrived, we tentatively sampled from them to determine what each plate held. Some of the dishes were readily identifiable, and with hilarious attempts at sign language and a chorus of sounds that represented a variety of animals and seafood, we put a label to each—with the exception of one. That platter held several relatively small pieces of meat. As people sampled the dish, they made their best guesses. The Vietnamese doctors offered no clues, so the guesses got wilder with each nibble. Someone across the table finally gave us a hint.

"Woof."

I should have had enough beer in me to minimize the effects of realizing I'd just eaten dog, but that wasn't the case. To me, the act smacked of cannibalism; I was dining with a group of people who didn't share my appreciation for canines. Of all of the things I'd witnessed while in Kuwait, Bangladesh, and Viet Nam, I found this act among the most disturbing. The thought of making a meal out of man's best friend turned my stomach.

Vietnam was, for me, the best mission AVMT had taken. The team, comprised of doctors and nurses with more experience than some of the other teams I'd traveled with, displayed a seriousness I'd not noted on other trips—maybe because of the nature of their fields and our location.

Cindy was different on that trip. Was it because the team of volunteers had more years of experience and a higher level of expertise? Was it that they weren't impressed by her wealth and position? Or could it have been that standing so close to where her husband had been captured and held for more than five years touched her heart?

I still don't know.

## Chapter 8

The contacts I made while working in the Government and International Affairs office at America West Airlines numbered among the job's many benefits. Because our office was involved with local, state, and federal governments, I met bureaucrats and elected officials at every level. Also, our office interacted with organizations not directly involved in the politics we wanted to influence.

One of those organizations was the Ronald Reagan Presidential Library Foundation in Los Angeles. I became friends with a few people who worked for the foundation, as well as with some of its board members. Originally, I had been contacted with a request to donate airline tickets for their people who traveled back and forth between Washington D.C. and Los Angeles, transporting papers and artifacts that eventually became part of the library's inventory.

On several occasions while in Los Angeles, I'd stop by President Reagan's offices in the Fox Tower to visit with his staff and, when the situation allowed, have a few short words with the President himself. One friend, John Lee, always made sure those handshakes took place; whenever possible, he'd introduce me to other dignitaries and board members who were in the offices during my visits. I met Lod Cook, chairman of Atlantic Richfield Company, and Charles and Mary Jane Wick. Mr. Wick was a member of Reagan's "kitchen cabinet," and Mrs. Wick served on the foundation board.

I worked with John to make sure America West's contribution was large enough to ensure its place on the major contributors' wall in the library's entry, while Mary Jane Wick and I often discussed other opportunities for involvement with the foundation over lunch.

After I left America West to work at the American Voluntary Medical Team, I maintained my friendships at the Reagan Foundation and with Mrs. Wick. I'd attended a few of the President's birthday parties, but I left America West prior to the library's opening and was afraid I'd miss the celebration. To my great delight, I received an invitation to the opening and a cocktail party the night prior at the Beverly Wilshire Hotel. In addition to tickets for my mother and me, John secured four more, which I asked him to extend to Marty Whalen and his wife—my boss from America West—and to John and Cindy McCain. John, for whatever reason, declined the invitation—we weren't aware he didn't plan to join us until we arrived at an airport near their home on Oak Creek, near Cottonwood, Arizona—but the rest of us flew to Los Angeles on Cindy's private plane and had a memorable time.

The evening prior to the library's opening, Cindy, Mom, and I attended a lavish reception at the Beverly Wilshire Hotel, where I had opportunity to visit with many friends from the Reagan Foundation and meet a variety of characters from politics and Hollywood. Prince Al Sabah also attended to represent the people of Kuwait, and I was thrilled to introduce Mom to him. Mom recognized old Hollywood stars I'd never heard of but who had been famous when she was a young girl. For both of us, it was a once-in-a-lifetime happening—indeed, a night to remember.

The next morning dawned bright and beautiful. The Whalens, Cindy, Mom, and I traveled in a stretch limousine from the Beverly Wilshire Hotel to the Reagan library in Simi Valley. I felt quite special, traveling in such a manner; but once we arrived at the library, I realized it was the transport of choice for everyone attending the celebration. Limousines of every make and model lined the hillside to the library's perching place. Dark suits seemed the choice for almost every man I saw, and most of the women wore conservative day suits.

The opening celebration was a beautiful display of pomp, but the entrance of five living presidents, walking side by side, impressed me most. Presidents Nixon, Ford, Carter, Reagan, and Bush all attended the ceremony that day, and I still treasure the photograph that I received from the foundation—the first picture in American history of five living presidents together.

It was an election year, and Cindy asked me to contact some of the people I knew in Reagan's office to see if the President would be available to speak at a fundraiser for John in Beverly Hills. It seemed odd to me that John didn't have his own contacts in the President's office, but I was happy to oblige. I've never understood why Senator McCain—if he cared about such contacts—didn't accept the invitation to attend the opening of the Reagan Library. In retrospect, I wonder if it might have been Cindy who wanted me to make the contact so she could offer my work to John's campaign as her contribution to the re-election efforts.

I knew Cindy wasn't a fan of Nancy Reagan. She'd stated many times that Mrs. Reagan had been rude because Cindy wore a red dress to a luncheon hosted by Mrs. Reagan. Red, of course, was Mrs. Reagan's signature color. I couldn't imagine a First Lady concerning herself with the dress color of a Congressman's wife, but Cindy stated it enough times and with enough conviction that I decided it must be true. (Years later, I learned that Mrs. Reagan might have been less-than-warm because Carol McCain, John's first wife, was a friend of the First Lady—and Cindy had been the mistress.)

I reached out to Mrs. Wick and asked if I could meet her to discuss the Reagans' appearance at the fundraiser. I knew she was a dear friend of Mrs. Reagan and might be able to influence the decision. Mary Jane agreed, and Cindy arranged for me to be flown to LAX in her private plane and shuttled around Los Angeles in a limousine to work out the details. By the end of the day, Mary Jane had assured me the Reagans would attend John's fundraiser. To make the most expedient use of time, I also met with personnel at the private club where the event would take place to discuss the menu and talked with a florist about flowers for the event.

Most in attendance at the thousand-dollar-per-plate dinner were Anheuser-Busch distributors from Southern California. Mrs. Reagan, wearing a copper colored brocade suit, appeared to be polite to Cindy, who, of course, wore a red dress. Cindy's parents flew in for the dinner, and I made sure Mary Jane Wick had a private moment with them to ask for a donation to the library foundation. It seemed to me a mutually beneficial evening.

Ironically, I wouldn't have participated in this event while working at America West. Employees were told if we ever worked on a political campaign, we'd have to do it as unpaid time off—be it hours or days or weeks—and it would need to be properly documented so it couldn't be misinterpreted as being done on company time. Perhaps because I was working for AVMT, a non-profit organization, the rules were different. Regardless of the reason, I was thankful to find no deductions from my paychecks for the time I spent working on the fundraiser.

## Chapter 9

On another occasion, the AVMT team took an exploratory trip to El Salvador. When we arrived in San Salvador, the capital, I was surprised by its normalcy in light of the twenty-year civil war that had left 70,000 dead and untold numbers missing and injured. Aircraft from several international carriers filled the tarmac, and the terminal, although dated, seemed like most terminals. Only a few of us made this preliminary trip. Cindy's diplomatic passport, as always, expedited our journey through Customs, and we soon headed to our hotel. On the way, I marveled at San Salvador's beautiful architecture, reminiscent of that of most Central American countries but enhanced by its lush location.

In line with our mission to address the medicals needs of the people, we visited a factory that made artificial limbs and then met with government leaders to determine where AVMT might be of use. Ultimately, it was determined that we would establish temporary clinics in two remote villages and provide general medical care for people who might not otherwise have access to those services.

During our short stay in San Salvador, riots broke out in South Central Los Angeles in response to the Rodney King beating, and we spent considerable time watching updates on CNN International. We could hardly imagine an American city under siege, and everyone became concerned about the return flight that would land in the middle of the conflict at

LAX. Some consolation came with knowledge that the short connection time would limit exposure to danger, and late evening would see most everyone safely at home in Phoenix.

About forty-five minutes prior to landing, a flight attendant approached our row in First Class, where I was seated next to Cindy. "Are you Mrs. McCain?" she asked.

"Yes, I am."

"The Captain would like to speak to you."

We looked at each other, but neither of us said anything as she left her seat and headed to the front of the plane. I couldn't imagine any plausible reason why the Captain would need to talk with a passenger—even if that passenger was Cindy McCain. Maybe he just knew she was onboard and wanted to pass along regards to her or the Senator.

I watched as Cindy followed the flight attendant to the front of the cabin and conversed with the pilot, who was waiting for her in the forward galley. Within minutes, Cindy returned to her seat and buckled herself in.

"What's going on?" I asked.

"People are shooting at planes at LAX, so the Captain's about to announce our flight is being diverted to San Diego."

"Wow. Things must be really bad." Feelings of unease traveled through me.

Ken leaned across the aisle and asked Cindy what was going on. She informed him of the situation.

"If we have to be diverted, San Diego is a good place to go because it will be easy to get back to Phoenix," I thought aloud. The America West segments of our trip had been donated, so I knew a few phone calls would get our group rerouted.

"I asked the Captain to contact Dalton and Martha. They'll pick us up in San Diego," Cindy said. Pilots Dalton and Martha flew the Hensleys' twin engine Beechcraft King Air 300 plane.

The Captain announced the diversion to the San Diego airport and assured passengers their transportation needs would be accommodated. The almost-quiet flight broke out in a buzz of conversations that speculated about the evening's events.

Within a short time, we'd landed and were taxiing toward the terminal. Because of the large number of jumbo jets that had been diverted to the airport, the gates couldn't handle the traffic. Planes parked and passengers deplaned wherever available paved surfaces could be located. To our relief, Dalton and Martha taxied the Hensley plane within yards of our aircraft, so we were soon wheels up and headed home to Phoenix.

Within a few weeks, we returned to El Salvador with a relatively small complement of doctors and nurses, a younger group than on previous trips. We traveled by cars and pick-ups to the small towns of El Transito and Puerto Parada. In both places we established small clinics, and the team members treated a variety of cases. Many people stood in line to see the doctors. They often didn't need medical attention, but simply wanted to be examined by American physicians, who spent lots of time listening to perfectly normal heart beats—there seemed to be a fascination with stethoscopes. Nurses cleaned wax from the ears of innumerable children.

In El Transito we slept on the floor of an open-air building made of brick and stucco —we felt a small earthquake while in that structure—and in Puerto Parada we slept on the floor of a garage-type structure, so space was tight. We carried portable showers with us, large black bladders that we hung in the sun to warm the water. Needless to say, this limited our opportunities to bathe.

Cindy did not seem to relate to some of the women on that trip and spent most of her time taking photographs with Ken. One day, while the others were out working in the clinic in Puerto Parada, she started to rifle through her bags.

"Some of the drugs are missing," she stated.

"What?" I wasn't sure I'd heard her correctly.

"Some of the drugs I was carrying in my bags are missing."

Because she always carried the narcotics in her own baggage, only she knew the types and quantities of the controlled substances she had in her possession. Again I questioned in my mind why she persisted in this practice. If the paperwork for those drugs was properly completed, there was no reason for her to carry them in her personal belongings.

Within a short period of time, she asked if one of the nurses seemed as though she might be high.

"I don't think so. She seems perfectly normal to me."

"There's something off about her." Cindy seemed to be daring me to challenge her.

"I've not noticed anything."

Cindy went on to tell Ken and a few others she was suspicious of the nurse's behavior and, in the same breath, mentioned the missing drugs. Ken agreed with Cindy's suspicions, but everyone else seemed uncomfortable about her less-than-subtle allegation. When no one other than Ken expressed concern about her claims, she eventually stopped speculating.

I don't believe the drugs were missing. Because no one but Cindy had access to the inventory, it would be hard to determine whether they were missing or not. I don't believe the nurse nor anyone else traveling as volunteers were responsible for the missing drugs, and my suspicions about the whereabouts of those drugs has never changed.

When we left El Salvador, I didn't return to Phoenix with the rest of the AVMT team. Cindy had asked that I go to Dhaka, Bangladesh, to handle some paperwork regarding Bridget's adoption. When we had passed through Houston on the way to San Salvador, I'd put a separate suitcase with fresh clothes in an airport locker. On the return flight, I sent my El Salvador bag on to Phoenix and collected the Bangladesh bag in Houston. From there I traveled to Los Angeles, stayed the night, and connected through Tokyo to Bangkok. After another overnight stay, I traveled the final leg of my journey to Dhaka.

Prior to the El Salvador trip, I'd contacted John Eaton, the General Manager of the Dhaka Sheraton whom I'd met on the first trip to Dhaka, and told him I'd be returning to Bangladesh and might need his assistance. Upon my arrival, he had a car waiting for me at the airport. When I reached the hotel, he informed me he and his wife wanted me to join them for a dinner party in their hotel apartment.

In addition to the Eatons and me, several people from the U.S. embassy also attended. During dinner, several of them discussed an American television magazine show that had featured a story about a young woman from Nebraska who'd embezzled millions of dollars from a New York City bank. Just before I departed for my El Salvador/Bangladesh trip, Mom told me a hometown girl who had attended the same church my family belonged to had been charged with embezzling from a New York bank. I suspected they were talking about the same person. Not wanting to be the guy that said, "I know her"—how weird would that have seemed, given we were on the opposite side of the earth?—I kept my mouth shut and simply nodded in recognition of the story they were telling. After returning to my room, I called Mom—I had no idea what time it was in Nebraska, but she sounded groggy when she answered the phone.

"Tom? Where are you?"

"I'm in Dhaka."

"Is everything ok?"

"Yes. Everything's fine. Guess who came up at dinner?"

"I have no idea."

"Everyone was talking about a show that featured a girl from Nebraska who'd embezzled millions of dollars from a New York bank."

"Did they mention her name?" she asked.

"No. But who else could it be?"

"You're right. That's funny." she said. "Did you say you know her?"

"No. They'd have thought I was crazy."

We talked a few more minutes, and then I went to bed early. It'd been a long trip from San Salvador to Dhaka, and I had lots of ground to cover in a short time.

The next morning, with assistance from John Eaton's secretary, I prepared a newspaper advertisement to run in local papers, announcing that a baby was to be adopted by an American family, and, should anyone wish to contest the adoption, they had a set amount of time to do so. Eaton's secretary also contacted advertising representatives that met me at the hotel and collected the money to pay for the legal notices. In addition to the newspaper ads, Cindy's adoption attorney had prepared documents that, if I could locate either of Bridget's parents, needed to be signed.

The second day of my stay in Dhaka, I returned to the orphanage where we'd found Bridget. After a few introductions and inquiries, the nuns advised me that Bridget's mother was still there. I was happy to have found her with so little hassle.

A woman of petite stature, she seemed pleased to learn where her daughter was, but she also seemed intimidated by the situation. I hoped the nuns explained the paper she was signing in a way that allowed her to understand it and that they were able to give her some sense of the privileged life Bridget would lead. I doubt they or Bridget's mother had any grasp of John McCain's stature or Cindy McCain's wealth, but I'm confident they understood she'd lead a better life than she'd have had in Bangladesh—and that she'd receive the treatment required to correct her cleft palate. After I'd obtained her mark and fingerprint, I asked the nuns about

Bridget's father. I understood them to say the baby was illegitimate and they had no knowledge of him. With that information, the ads I'd placed, and the "signature" I'd acquired, I had enough documentation to return to Phoenix.

On my long flight back, I spent considerable time processing everything I knew about the McCains. While my opinion of them had deteriorated, I was sure they would provide Bridget a life beyond anything the little girl's biological mother could offer or even comprehend.

Beyond that, I tried to come to grips with the uncomfortable feeling that all was not as it should be. Little things kept nagging at my mind—Cindy's disappearance for days at a time, her failure to keep scheduled appointments that made Kathy the scapegoat for event planners' wrath, her blatant disregard for Kathy's feelings and loyalty, her determination to keep Bridget despite the "rule" that didn't permit her to take the baby permanently out of the country. Certainly, Bridget's life was far better because of the adoption, but that wasn't the point—it was the misleading way she had done it. I wondered about John's extended absences from home and his apparent disinterest in what his wife was doing. And why he had declined an invitation to the Reagan Library opening, after which I was requested to use my contacts to arrange for President Reagan to attend his political fundraiser? The list went on and on. What had I gotten myself into when I went to work for AVMT?

# Chapter 10

One of the perks of immense wealth is house staff, and Cindy had plenty of both. A core of workers always seemed in abundance—a man and wife who were in charge of the Phoenix house and its grounds, the man that worked at the Phoenix house but was also responsible for the Oak Creek home, nannies that came and went, and others who were brought in on a temporary basis.

The McCains had three common children—Meghan, Jack and Jimmy—and John had grown children from his marriage to his first wife, Carol. I don't recall Cindy's mentioning John's other children but, given her attitude toward her own step-siblings, she may not have considered them part of her family. (Both of Cindy's parents had a child from previous relationships.) At that time, Meghan, the oldest, was probably of kindergarten age and the boys were yet too young to attend school.

When I started visiting the McCain house, one nanny, Teresa, appeared to be in charge of the youngsters. I remember thinking those three small children had busier schedules than I did, but the hustle and bustle never seemed to faze Teresa.

A nice person—though not necessarily gregarious—she always focused on the kids, at least from my perspective. I'd known of her family from Marty Whalen, my boss at America West. If I recall correctly, her father was involved in Phoenix's East Valley politics and was well-known and respected in the

Mesa area. Whenever I saw her, she was dressed in casual slacks and a top that complimented her large frame and athletic build. Her blonde, simply-styled hair looked effortless, and her facial structure and skin didn't need makeup. I don't know whether the time she spent studying to be a nun influenced the way she dressed or it was simply her style. We visited on numerous occasions, and I found her engaging; however, many of our conversations were cut short because she had to tend to the children.

Because of the positive impression I had of her, I was stunned the morning Cindy called me at the office from her home.

"Goose, you'll never guess what happened."

"Maybe not."

"I had to fire Teresa. She molested Meghan!"

"What! Teresa, the *nanny*?"

"Yes, the police are here now."

"What are they doing?"

"They're interviewing Meghan."

"Where's Teresa? What can I do?" I couldn't help but think there was more to the story.

"She's not here. I'm not sure where she is."

"Did you witness something?"

"I've got to go. They need to talk to me." She was gone.

I sat at my desk and contemplated the situation. I'd still not resolved in my mind Cindy's repeated inferences that one of the nurses had stolen drugs while we were in El Salvador or Kathy's concerns about discrepancies in AVMT's inventory. And now this—an allegation of molestation. It was a stretch to imagine that these occurrences were linked, but it was also difficult for me to believe they were coincidental. My gut instincts screamed that something was wrong—maybe more than one "something."

Dreadful as it is to contemplate, a sexual abuse incident could have taken place, I suppose; but with all the people who went through the McCain house every day, little opportunity for such an occurrence existed. Also, I believe anyone who knew Teresa would feel her personal character wouldn't allow her to treat a child in any other than a loving way. Could Cindy's allegation have been motivated by something else? Were the allegations surrounding AVMT's drug inventories somehow tied to the Teresa story? The thought terrified me.

I spoke to Cindy a few more times that day, and she continued to make horrific claims about Teresa.

"How's Meghan?" I asked.

"She's fine."

*How could a child who had just endured the trauma of sexual abuse be fine?* Cindy's tone didn't allow for additional questions. Her baffling behavior and responses suggested to me that she was more concerned with the destruction of Teresa's character than the welfare of her daughter.

In my mind I kept coming back to the same questions: Could Cindy have mishandled the controlled drugs belonging to AVMT? Might she have a dependency on prescription drugs? Could Teresa have confronted her on this matter?

If Cindy was suffering from addiction to prescription drugs, I realized she needed help. Unfortunately, I didn't know how to approach a boss and offer that help or how to tactfully suggest professional intervention.

Things hadn't turned out as I'd hoped at AVMT. I wasn't always confident of our mission, and I felt the organization needed stronger leadership. However, I didn't wish any ill will on AVMT or Cindy. She and I had become good friends. Although it was at times difficult to be her friend, I still believed her motivations and heart were in the right place in wanting to provide needed medical services to victims of wars and natural disasters.

For the next few days, Cindy continued to talk about the alleged molestation incident. Her audience—Kathy, Jeri, Tracy, and I—sat in silence as she went on her rants. I don't believe any of us thought the allegations had merit. I know I didn't.

A few days later, without Cindy's knowledge, I called Teresa.

"Hey, Teresa. It's Tom."

"Hi, Tom."

I tried to put her at ease. "You don't need to say anything in response to what I'm about to say."

"Okay."

"I don't believe Cindy. If there is anything I can do, please let me know."

"Thanks, Tom." Her voice was soft.

"Call me at home if you need anything." I gave her my home telephone number.

"I will."

After a few months—other than when she used Meghan's alleged molestation as an excuse for not attending a meeting or an event—Cindy rarely mentioned Teresa or the situation. During that time period, I learned that the police investigation of Cindy's allegation came up empty—they would not press charges. Unfortunately, I doubt that was any great relief to Teresa. Her credibility and reputation had been ruined.

Prior to Teresa's termination, I'd told Cindy about a nanny agency in Nebraska that my mom had mentioned to me. Once Teresa was gone, she asked that I get her contact information. I did. A few days later, she called me.

"Goose, can you help me with that nanny agency?"

"What do you need?"

"I completed the application and returned it to them, but they want me to provide names of my former nannies so they can contact them as references."

"That seems reasonable."

"I'm a U.S. Senator's wife. That should be reference enough."

"I'll see what I can do."

I never contacted the agency because I didn't think it was my place to suggest they suspend their standard application procedures for Cindy. I'd provided the name of the agency, and that was all I was willing to do. However, someone must have caved to Cindy's demands—or Cindy provided them with the names of nannies that had remained friendly with her—because within weeks a new nanny arrived.

Months later, at the Coffee Plantation, a coffee shop a few blocks from my condo, I ran into Teresa. We exchanged smiles and a few pleasant words, but that was the extent of our encounter. She appeared to have lost weight and no longer carried an athletic posture. To me, she looked broken.

(Years passed before I heard anything more about Teresa. In 2008, a reporter who contacted me said she'd gone to speak to Teresa at her job—a convenience store in Mesa—but when Teresa realized she was there to speak about the McCains, she broke into tears and ran to the back room. The Teresa I'd met many years prior would have never run from a question, but would've given an honest, thoughtful response.)

In the midst of all the goings-on at the McCain house, Kathy received numerous calls from doctors who had traveled with AVMT on its expeditions, questioning why Cindy had contacted them about using their Drug Enforcement Administration (DEA) numbers so she could acquire drugs for future AVMT trips. Cindy hadn't told Kathy she'd been calling doctors, so Kathy did not know what Cindy's plans were for the drugs. Also, Kathy said that, based on inventory, she wasn't aware we needed the pharmaceuticals in question. Everyone seemed uneasy with the situation, and we discussed it openly among ourselves.

Because Kathy served as Cindy's personal secretary, her desk was located just outside Cindy's office at Hensley & Co.

AVMT's suite of offices was located in the same building, but around the corner and down the hall. Kathy often spent time at Cindy's desk, organizing her mail and preparing her calendar. (AVMT had moved from its downtown location to the Hensley & Co. building to reduce costs and to accommodate Kathy's job as Cindy's secretary in both capacities.) While working at Cindy's desk, she told us she had discovered something odd: a number of doctors' names and DEA numbers had been written on a piece of paper that was lying out in the open. The file containing that information was supposed to be kept locked.

No one seemed to know what Cindy might be doing with the names and numbers and how she might be involving those doctors. It seemed improbable that any of them would knowingly provide her with drugs, but enough inexplicable things had happened that our imaginations began to run wild.

As our discussions about the craziness at AVMT became more frequent, the girls relayed details I had never heard. Kathy and Jeri, because of their history with Cindy and the Hensleys, possessed a wealth of knowledge. Kathy seemed very familiar with all Cindy's goings on, professional and personal; and Jeri, who had dinner with the Hensleys almost every night, shared stories from her parents' perspective. At times, I wanted to chuckle—had it not been for the seriousness of the issue, I might have—because Kathy and Jeri seemed to compete for the dubious distinction of sharing the best and juiciest details.

During one of these discussions, Jeri told us that Cindy's parents intended to confront her about her erratic behavior. I don't know that they were aware she might have problems with prescription drugs. Perhaps Jeri had mentioned the AVMT staff's concerns so they wanted to discuss what she had shared. Or maybe they had witnessed behavior they couldn't understand. We could only hope an intervention might make things better.

I never noticed a positive change in Cindy's behavior, nor was she ever absent for an extended period of time. It seemed the hoped-for intervention didn't happen.

# Chapter 11

Cindy asked me to prepare AVMT for a trip to Florida in response to the devastation caused by Hurricane Andrew. I contacted Marty Whalen to arrange transportation through America West; and Kathy, Tracy, and I worked with local grocery chains to secure pallets of non-perishable foods and supplies. A plea for people in Phoenix to make personal contributions of the same sort went out through local television and radio stations. The outpouring of contributions was overwhelming, and the task of getting everything to Florida became monumental.

Again, I contacted Marty, this time about transporting the cargo. I also made arrangements with UPS to handle the transportation of the supplies from Orlando to Miami, where it would be distributed.

Cindy, always aware of a photo opportunity, wanted people traveling with AVMT to wear hospital scrubs. I'd not been to a hurricane-ravaged area, but I'd seen the damage caused by tornadoes. The thought of digging through piles of rubble in flimsy hospital scrubs seemed unrealistic, even irresponsible. I thought it ridiculous to not allow the team to wear clothes made of heavier materials—but Cindy insisted on the scrubs.

With the exception of the huge amount of supplies, the trip to Florida was the least effective AVMT venture. Local hospitals handled the large number of patients, and clean-up hadn't started because damage assessments hadn't been completed.

* * * * *

Overlapping the tragedy in Florida was a man-made tragedy in Somalia. Refugees weren't able to get the medical care they needed, so Cindy decided that would be AVMT's next destination. Her sense of adventure made my job fun, as well as hazardous. She and I shared a screwed-up sense of fun, but this trip pushed my limits. Mark Salter, a man from John McCain's office who often consulted with us about foreign trips, advised us that conditions in Somalia were very dangerous. Ken Akers, Cindy's confidant and an equally crazy thrill-seeker, supported the notion of a trip, and the two of them decided we should be suited in bulletproof vests and carry guns.

I don't support the use of firearms, so Cindy and Ken's idea made no sense to me. Also, I don't know how she thought we would transport guns to Somalia. Maybe she intended to use her diplomatic passport to go through Customs just as she did when we transported regulated narcotics. Fortunately—perhaps because of Cindy's unwillingness to deal with her drug consumption, her obvious unraveling, and the increasing concern of her parents for her welfare—the trip to Somalia never happened.

Thank God. The last thing I wanted to learn was how to handle a gun.

## Chapter 12

By the time we returned from Florida, it was obvious to me—and seemed to be to the others in the office—that Cindy was out of control. Her extreme mood swings and her inability to stay focused on a single project made working for her almost impossible. The trip to Somalia was forgotten as quickly as it had been suggested, and the AVMT staff continued to suffer from a lack of leadership and clearly defined goals.

Ken and Cindy spent considerable time sorting through the thousands of photographs Ken had taken on AVMT's various missions to pick the best images for a calendar. Nobody other than the two of them knew the status of the calendar until one day it appeared on my desk for proofing. The first thing that caught my eye was the overly ornate font used for the text, not the hauntingly beautiful photographs that seemed to focus on the huge, dark eyes of a malnourished child or the strength and conviction of an elderly person who appeared on the brink of collapse. Somehow Ken captured the pain and the beauty of each of his subjects.

AVMT, from the time I began working there, had used a specific font on all its printed materials because I felt consistency was important for the "branding" of the organization. I leafed through the calendar month by month and was impressed by the beautiful photographs but distracted by the feminine font.

The following morning, I called Ken.

"Hey, Ken. It's Tom."

"What's up, Tom?"

"I want to discuss the calendar. I love the pictures—they're beautiful—but the font isn't the one we use."

"Really?"

"We use the same font on all our materials. Sorry if nobody told you."

"Cindy already approved the calendar. It was sent to the printer days ago."

"I just got the proof yesterday." Why was the proof on my desk at this late date? I knew that debating the issue of the font would go nowhere. Ken and Cindy had always been tight, and it wasn't his fault I wasn't in the loop at a time when corrections could have been made. "Then I guess that's the font we'll go with."

A few weeks prior to the calendar incident, Cindy had asked me to talk to Ken about cutting his photography fees in half from $500 per day to $250. In addition to Ken's daily fee, all his expenses and production and printing costs were paid. Given the volume of photographs Ken took on every trip, it's hard to imagine the amount of money he received over the years.

My conversation with Ken regarding his fees didn't go well; I'd not anticipated it would. Rather than settling the issue with me, Ken later called to tell me he'd gone to Cindy. According to him, she said I was trying to find ways to save AVMT money and suggested we might reduce his fee. He also told me she thought his work was important to AVMT's success, and he would continue to receive his $500 fee and all his expenses.

I was disappointed, sad, and confused that Cindy hadn't backed me up on the issues of the font and Ken's daily fees. Reducing his fee, after all, had been her idea, not mine. Even more, I didn't understand why she appeared to have set me up for failure with Ken. I didn't want to be part of her game—she seemed to enjoy setting people up for confrontation—nor did I want to lose credibility with Ken because I knew, as long as I worked at AVMT, I would need to find a way to work with him.

The number of unresolved issues within AVMT seemed to be growing in direct proportion to the dwindling of my ability to manage them. The protections I had enjoyed while working within the corporate environment of America West no longer existed. In their place, I found myself vulnerable to Cindy's emotional whims. Some days, everything at work seemed to progress at a controlled, fluid pace; other days, the lack of structure and leadership seemed to jerk the organization around as if it was an engine sputtering for its last gulp of gas.

On the whole, AVMT appeared to be headed downhill. Although it might be perceived as less than professional, Kathy, Tracy, Jeri, and I had many conversations about the organization's future. The calls Kathy had received from doctors, questioning why Cindy wanted to use their DEA numbers to obtain drugs, and her concerns about the discrepancies in AVMT's pharmaceutical inventory had apparently led to a Drug Enforcement Administration investigation.

Kathy and Dalton Smith—I never figured out why the Hensleys' pilot was involved—worked several days to prepare AVMT's inventory for inspection by the DEA. Even though legitimate reasons existed to question AVMT's inventory and record keeping, Kathy reported that Cindy said the whole thing might be politically motivated—someone was trying to make trouble for John in his re-election year.

Before becoming aware of Cindy's drug habit, I'd wondered why she paid retail prices for drugs needed to maintain AVMT's inventory. Because AVMT operated as a non-profit organization, pharmaceutical companies could have donated drugs. At the very least, they would likely have agreed to sell them to us at wholesale prices. The whole scenario made no financial sense for an organization that needed to keep a careful eye on budget.

"Why are we paying retail prices for drugs?" I asked Kathy. By then I knew the answer, but I wanted to know if another element played into the picture.

"We always have," Kathy replied.

"That's stupid. We could get them for free if we asked."

"Cindy thinks it's easier this way."

Her response almost knocked me off my chair. The wheels began turning. Carefully controlled substances were slipping through our inventory at an alarming rate. Could purchasing drugs from local, friendly pharmacies allow Cindy to circumvent the rules placed on pharmaceutical companies to record the transfer of narcotics from their inventories to AVMT's?

"That's a lot of prescriptions. Is she having them written in her name?" I suddenly needed to know exactly what was going on.

"She's had prescriptions written in *all* our names," Kathy said.

"*What*? She'd better not have had prescriptions written in *my* name."

Kathy raised her eyebrows as if to confirm my concern.

"You'd be surprised to know everyone she's involved," said Jeri.

"Who's writing the prescriptions?" I asked.

"Max. Maybe others," Kathy answered.

"How can they do that without our permission?"

"Cindy's told them it's for AVMT's inventory."

"And no one's asking any questions?" The implications of the situation hit me hard. "Who else is involved?"

Kathy went on to relate that she'd received calls from doctors, in particular Tom Moffo, saying that AVMT wasn't to use his DEA number to obtain drugs. She said she wasn't sure how it was being done, but she knew Cindy had access to the files that contained the doctors' DEA numbers and their signatures. All this seemed incredulous—beyond belief—but how else could she obtain drugs, using their DEA numbers without involving them directly?

Kathy and Jeri told us they thought Cindy had used all our names and that they knew Dr. Johnson, for one, had written prescriptions. They feared Cindy had put all of us at risk.

"She better not screw this up. It'd be bad politics in an election year to have a bunch of disgruntled employees who know about the Senator's wife with a drug habit that's put them all in jeopardy." I scowled.

"I know Jimmy and Smitty are concerned," Jeri said. "This is killing them."

"What are they going to do? What is John going to do?" I asked.

"I don't think they'll do anything until after the election," Jeri replied.

"How can they not?" I wondered aloud.

I suddenly felt very vulnerable, and I believe the others did, too. We all depended on our jobs for income. If Cindy compromised our livelihoods to feed her personal drug habit or jeopardized the futures of the doctors that worked with AVMT, we'd all suffer—as would the many people whose lives we touched on AVMT missions. Kathy probably had the most at risk because her job provided insurance coverage for her family. But neither Tracy nor I had a person in our lives who brought in a second income. Jeri may have been the least vulnerable.

"Do you think John knows?" I asked.

No one answered.

If we, her coworkers, recognized Cindy's addiction, how could her husband *not* know? Yes, they led separate lives, but it seemed improbable that he wouldn't at some point take note of her obvious behavior changes.

I thought it pathetic that a woman with all the trappings of the world didn't have anyone in her life who would react proactively to her self-destructive behavior. Perhaps her parents lacked the strength to confront her—I don't know their reason. If John did suspect her addiction, it appeared as though he chose to not deal with it. Or maybe he didn't want to make it an issue prior to the election. Of course, we had no way of determining what went on behind closed doors.

I still don't know who knew what and when. Because of her husband's regular, scheduled absences, Cindy may have been able to hide her addiction from him for an extended period of time. Not so with her house and office staff. *We* knew. I felt certain her household staff also knew. However, her wealth did give her an edge over the less affluent junkie; she could obtain her drugs in a more sophisticated manner—through doctors, pharmacies, and her non-profit organization. Regardless of the manner, however, it was wrong. Furthermore, she was apparently making me a party to her game by using my name to feed her habit. *That* could not continue.

When Kathy informed us that she'd been contacted by the DEA and they'd asked for a complete inventory of AVMT drugs—about the same time Dr. Moffo approached her concerning the unauthorized use of his DEA number—I began to question my decision to join AVMT. During my employment, I had avoided the inventorying of drugs; pill counting sounded quite monotonous. Later, I was relieved I'd never been involved in that process. My only knowledge of that phase of the organization came through Kathy. However, she seemed very concerned about the DEA's audits and her conversations with Dr. Moffo.

As more and more information surfaced, it became increasingly difficult to accept Cindy's dismissal of the audit as an attempt to discredit her family in an election year. We never heard anything from John McCain's office regarding the possibility of political attacks; and in the end, no one appeared to believe her story, which appeared to be yet another of Cindy's accusations.

"Kathy, what will you do about the discrepancies in the inventory?" I asked.

"I can't be responsible for the inventory. Cindy keeps some of the drugs at the house, so I've never entered them into the inventory."

"*Why* does she keep AVMT's drugs at the house?"

"I don't know. She just does."

I never learned where AVMT's drugs were kept at Hensley & Company. Kathy and Dalton had always done the inventory work, and at some point I believe Dr. Johnson may have helped them—I'm not aware to what extent. Regardless of who was involved, there was no *justifiable* reason for Cindy to have kept any quantity of drugs that should have been in AVMT's inventory in her home.

Kathy's stress during the audit was palpable, and I don't recall that Cindy was ever present. The burden of rectifying AVMT's records rested solely on Kathy's shoulders.

When faced with no other explanation for the missing pharmaceuticals, I accepted that Cindy took drugs from AVMT's inventory and had at least one doctor write prescriptions in other peoples' names—people who weren't aware until later that their names had been used to obtain drugs. I had no proof she had involved me, but I knew, to protect myself and others, I needed to take appropriate measures—yet I wasn't sure what those measures should be.

"Can you imagine what would happen should any of this be made public?" I tried to sound hypothetical rather than threatening.

"I know Jimmy would shut down AVMT," Jeri responded.

"What would we do?" Tracy asked.

I nodded. "We'd all find new jobs."

Kathy said nothing.

"I can't imagine the Hensleys letting it come to that," I said. "There's too much at stake." Even as I spoke, I wondered whether that was wishful thinking on my part.

## Chapter 13

"Oh, my god." I said it loud enough for Jeri, Kathy and Tracy to hear. "You'll never guess what she's done now."

The women were at my office door within seconds.

"Melinda, the adoption attorney, just called and told me Cindy said Bridgette's father was killed in a rickshaw accident."

"What?" all three asked simultaneously.

"Yeah. She called me to prep me for the adoption hearing, and she asked me about the father's death in the accident."

"That's crazy," Jeri said.

"I thought so," I replied.

"What did you tell her?" Tracy asked.

"I told her I have no knowledge of the father's death."

"You're the one who went there to finish the paperwork," Jeri said. "You should know."

I couldn't imagine why Cindy had felt it necessary to embellish the truth. Bridgette's story didn't need to be fluffed; its beauty stood on its own. Cindy had found the baby in an orphanage in Dhaka and had brought her back to the States to have her severe cleft palate corrected and the McCains intended to pursue adoption to give her a life she'd never have had in Bangladesh.

"Hang on. I'm going to call Cindy," I said.

The girls stood around my desk in silence.

"Hey, Cindy, it's Tom."

"Hey, Goose."

"I just got off of the phone with Melinda."

"She's nice, isn't she?"

"She seems nice enough." I paused for a moment. "Cindy, Melinda thinks Bridgette's father was killed in a rickshaw accident."

One of the girls snickered softly.

"I don't know where she came up with that," Cindy said.

"Hmm. I can't testify to that because, as far as I know from my conversation with the nuns, Bridgette's father was absent when she was born. Not dead."

"You should say whatever you need to for the hearing to go smoothly," Cindy responded.

The conversation was over. I sat motionless in disbelief.

"I know what happened," one of the girls said.

"What?" we asked in unison.

"The dad was peddling the rickshaw, and the mom was in back holding Bridgette. The dad gets hit by a truck, dies, and the baby flies from the mom's arms and splits her lip!"

We all roared with laughter and continued to add to the story to make it funnier and funnier. All these years later, I find it difficult to imagine how we found humor in such a stupid story, but at that moment, it was the comic relief we needed.

I called Melinda back. "I know you were told Bridgette's father was killed in a rickshaw accident, but I have no knowledge of that so I can't testify to it."

"What did they tell you at the orphanage?" Melinda asked.

"Not much. I was able to get the mother's 'X' and a finger print for the paperwork I had. When I asked about the father, I understood the nuns to say Bridgette was an illegitimate baby and they had no knowledge about the father or his whereabouts."

"That seems good enough," Melinda said.

"It has to be."

Around the office we continued to laugh about rickshaw accidents. My questions about the source of Cindy's information—or suspicions regarding the workings of her imagination—didn't matter. The adoption would proceed without a hitch. Regardless of Cindy's exaggerations, Bridgette would have a wonderful life.

When it came time for the adoption hearing, I was asked to be present and told I might be called upon as a witness. The proceeding was short. I think the judge was struck by the presence of a U.S. Senator and his wife in his courtroom, so the questions were general in nature. I wasn't asked to testify to anything about the father.

Shortly after Bridgette's adoption, John won his re-election to the U.S. Senate. I attended his election party at the McCain's Phoenix home and remember an abundance of McCain aides, members of the Arizona's Republican Party, and several supporters. Once the election was wrapped up, John and Cindy took a month-long vacation.

Upon her return from their holiday, she announced she wanted a small group to travel to India to "observe" conditions there. I'd been on enough "observation" trips to conclude that they produced little useable information. In fact, I believed those trips took assets away from the people who needed them in order to pay the expenses of the observers. I can't recall any information we collected that couldn't have been gathered from CNN or some other global news organization. John's office frequently scheduled meetings for AVMT with members of the host nation's health ministry or the equivalent; most of those meetings consisted of a handshake and a photograph. Cindy, however, always seemed to have a predetermined plan of action for AVMT that didn't accommodate the requests of government representatives.

Of course, those trips were always fun because they seemed like big adventures into exotic regions. For the India trip, Cindy wanted Tracy, Ken Akers, Max Johnson, and me to accompany her. I don't remember whether Max made the trip, but a few days before our scheduled departure, Cindy told me I would be staying in Phoenix to work on our program with the Navajo Nation in northern Arizona. I'd looked forward to visiting India but thought my work with the Navajos would be more beneficial—staying behind didn't bother me.

One day after the group left, I received a call.

"Hey, Tom, it's Cindy."

"Hi, Cindy. How's India?"

"Tom, I hear you've been talking about me."

I knew better than to respond.

"Yeah, someone told me you've been talking about me," she repeated.

I remained silent.

"I'll talk to you when I get back."

"Have a safe flight," I said.

I'll never know who told Cindy I was talking about her. All of us in the office had discussed her crazy behavior and the missing drugs. All of us had said we thought Cindy should be careful in her handling of us because we'd observed so much. All of us had talked about how she treated people. All of us were culpable when it came to office gossip.

I suspect, because of the small size of the India group and the intimacy it might have supported, someone may have innocently mentioned, perhaps even to Ken, about talk regarding Cindy's drug abuse. Ken may have then shared that information with Cindy. This is speculation, of course.

I didn't think much more about the angry call. We'd become so accustomed to Cindy's volatile temper that I assumed it would pass. However, the election was over, John had returned to Washington, and she seemed to be up to her old ways. My assumption could not have been more wrong.

Shortly after Cindy's return, she summoned me to her office. I should have been suspicious because she was actually *in* the office—along with Hensley & Company's bookkeeper. A warning shiver crept up my spine. I ignored it. Then she handed me my termination letter. Of the four of us—Kathy, Jeri, Tracy, and me—who had discussed Cindy's obvious drug habit and its detrimental effects on AVMT, I had apparently been deemed the biggest troublemaker and, therefore, the most expendable. I was stunned, but also hurt and happy and angry and hopeful all at the same time.

Stifling the inclination to speak in my defense, I bit my tongue. If I'd started to talk, I wouldn't have stopped before saying way too much. Ending up like Teresa didn't appeal to me, and I'd seen enough of Cindy's behavior to know that could happen. After returning to my office, I told the girls I'd been terminated. To my surprise and relief, I maintained my composure.

When I got home that night and had time to process what had happened, I realized I was a victim of my own bad decisions. I'd allowed myself to be defined by a job, and I'd allowed my job to define my life. I also realized how uncomfortable I'd been from the beginning of my tenure with AVMT. I chastised myself for my failure to see Cindy's issues when, in hindsight, I'd known on some level after our first meeting that things were not as they seemed.

Most of all, I realized my forced separation from AVMT was the best thing that could have happened to me.

# Chapter 14

After AVMT moved from its downtown Phoenix location to the Hensley headquarters, I had opportunity to become friends with Jimmy Hensley, Cindy's father. He was a large but not overweight man with silver-white hair, bright blue eyes, and a gentle personality. Most mornings, you could find him in the break room, having coffee with some of his company's executives. He always greeted me with a pleasant smile and an engaging comment.

A proud and honorable man, he showed his affection for Cindy in the sparkle of his eyes when he mentioned her; and his love for Smitty Hensley—his wife—was obviously abundant. Although it appeared he wasn't needed to monitor the company's day-to-day operations, his almost-daily presence seemed to influence the company's dynamic in a positive direction.

Hidden behind Jimmy Hensley's teddy-bear façade lay a determined man. He was a decorated soldier in World War II—a B-17 bombardier who was awarded the Distinguished Flying Cross. A hard worker with an eye firmly set on success, Jimmy became one of the wealthiest men in Arizona.

One day, while I was still employed by AVMT, Jimmy asked me to come to his office. When I arrived at the huge, handsomely appointed space, we engaged in perfunctory small talk before he got to the point of our meeting. He intended to take his management and sales staffs on a golf weekend to Mexico and asked if I could use my contacts at America West to secure a jet charter. Of course, I was more than happy to assist. Despite my differences with his daughter, I still considered Jimmy a friend.

Jimmy asked about AVMT in general terms and stated he'd not seen much of Cindy, so he wasn't aware of what was going on. He asked some probing questions but avoided any that might reveal answers he didn't want to hear. I felt sure he knew I was aware of Cindy's drug abuse, and I'd hoped we might in some way acknowledge our mutual concerns. To my disappointment the subject never came up.

I began organizing the charter and, after several phone calls and a few meetings, arranged for an America West flight to Mexico for Jimmy and his guests. When I informed him that everything had been taken care of, he invited me to fly with the group to ensure all went smoothly.

After Cindy fired me, Jimmy asked whether I would be willing to stick to our agreement and accompany him and the Hensley executives on the flight to Mexico—I said I'd be happy to. The loss of one relationship shouldn't dictate the loss of another, I reasoned. Besides, I liked the connection with Jimmy and believed he was a good man. He and I sat next to each other during the flight, and he voiced concern about my job search and my future plans. He even asked if he could do anything to help me. I didn't want to burden him with my thoughts about his daughter or my precarious situation, so I said I was confident about my job opportunities—but I'd appreciate using a computer and printer at AVMT to prepare my résumé. Without hesitation, he agreed to my request.

I'd not known how Jimmy felt about me following my firing, so it was heartening to hear he was concerned about my job prospects and willing to assist me as I prepared to search for work. Use of a computer and printer seemed a small request to make of a man of significant wealth, but it satisfied an immediate need so I could proceed with the task at hand. Jimmy's willingness to help reinforced my positive impressions of him.

Upon my return from Mexico, I contacted Kathy, told her Jimmy had said I could use a computer, and asked when it would be convenient for me to have access. Kathy told me she'd talk to Cindy and get back to me. Late the following afternoon, she called to tell me Cindy didn't agree with her father's offer. I wasn't welcome at AVMT.

Just as I had suspected, the gracious content of my termination letter was not sincere. In it, she had praised my work ethics and my contribution to the organization. However, denying me use of a computer to help me seek work revealed a different mindset—a vindictiveness that had not previously reared its head.

My mom bought me a computer and printer to help in my preparation of job search materials, and I sent out dozens of letters and résumés. I received very few responses and didn't know whether or not to be concerned because I'd never been involved in job hunting. Every job I'd worked in my adult life had come about because of circumstance—either I'd known someone who offered me a job or I stumbled upon a situation that seemed a natural progression in my career path. Of course, I needed to find another position; but I didn't know what new path I wanted to take. Nor did I know where to start. I did, however, want to return to an environment where employees were guaranteed those securities provided to workers within a corporate structure.

Although listing AVMT as an employer did not make me comfortable, I didn't want a gap in my employment history. Still, I debated whether the gap or the potential for a negative reference would be the most damaging.

While searching for a job, my thoughts often returned to AVMT, Cindy McCain, and the whole missing drugs debacle. Based on the pattern I'd witnessed of character assassination and false accusations, I couldn't help but conclude I might well be next. I remembered how devastated Teresa had been when accused of molesting Cindy's daughter. The finger-pointing and innuendos over missing drugs and a volunteer nurse during one of AVMT's humanitarian trips remained fresh in my mind. I can't say for sure whether Cindy's drug abuse was solely responsible for her care-less, cover-up manifesto, but I didn't want to be indicted for drugs gone missing. I needed to protect myself.

After a few weeks of contemplation and playing out what-if scenarios in my mind, I decided to speak to someone with knowledge of drug law. Specifically, I worried about my culpability should it be discovered that I had suspected Cindy's illegal drug activities and ignored them. Yet, if I contacted local officials or even state authorities, would my conversation be held in confidence? In my opinion, the only option was to contact the feds.

Tim, the brother of a friend, worked for the DEA. Although I didn't know him or his position within that organization, I thought it might be a good place to start. I asked my friend to have his brother call me. We made arrangements to meet.

As the appointment time approached, I fretted over the best way to present myself and tell my story. My credibility might be questioned, so I wanted to keep my statements succinct. I needed to be honest and forthright, but also to guard my words because I didn't know the legal ramifications of making a misstatement, even if it were an innocent failure to recall an incident exactly.

After stewing over potential scenarios for hours, I decided to present my story as a hypothetical situation and not tell Tim the name of the person I believed to be participating in illegal drug activity. I assumed his brother had told him what I had shared about Cindy's drug addiction, but I myself wasn't yet prepared to tell him.

My nervousness grew by the minute, and I fussed with things in the condo—straightening pictures and fluffing pillows. I rehearsed my lines and made a pitcher of tea, but wasn't sure it would be appropriate to offer it. I rehearsed my lines again.

The doorbell rang. I didn't want to seem overly anxious or too cool about the meeting, so I answered it at what I perceived to be the right moment. I'd not met Tim face to face, so I had no notion of the person I would be greeting. When I opened the door, two men holding DEA badges at my eye level stood in front of me. Tim introduced himself first; then Tom, the other agent, introduced himself. Casually dressed in jeans and polo shirts, they exhibited a friendly countenance and a laid-back attitude. I directed them up the flight of stairs to my dining room and invited both men to sit down while I got us all something to drink. Neither took an immediate seat, but instead perused the photographs of several dignitaries that hung on an adjacent wall. I returned with glasses of iced tea and we all sat down.

"That's an impressive wall." Tom gestured to the pictures.

"Thanks."

I'd often considered my picture wall—I called it my vanity wall—to be almost obnoxious; but given the conversation I was about to have, I hoped it might provide me some credibility. There were a few pictures with me with the McCains; two with Vice President Quayle; several with me and President Reagan; and my favorite one of me, my mother, Margaret Thatcher, and President and Mrs. Reagan.

"You know all those people?" Tom asked.

"I've met them." Under different circumstances I might have provided some background information about each picture. At that moment, however, it didn't seem fitting.

After more small talk, I clumsily transitioned to my carefully rehearsed story. Because I intentionally withheld names

and specific details, my story was laced with numerous varia-
tions of "if one knows" and questions about what one should
do if such a hypothetical situation did, in fact, exist. Both
men took notes and nodded their heads from time to time.
Tim appeared to lean forward as the meeting progressed
while Tom remained more rigid. While I talked, I watched
for them to look to each other or roll their eyes, but the only
thing I could discern was that they were well-trained to not
react.

I concluded my story by not wrapping it up or offering
next steps. I just stopped talking and looked to the agents as
if to say, "Do you want to know the specifics?"

I was embarrassed to think how many times I had gone
over this meeting in my mind and now that my presentation
was done, I didn't recall any portion of what I had mentally
prepared. I didn't want to know what these men thought of
me—nut job, quack, mental case—and was suddenly eager
for the meeting to conclude.

Tim stated that, given the hypothetical story, I was proper in coming forward. Then he urged me to name the person
I suspected of being involved in illegal drug activity.

Silence hung over the room like a dark cloud on a dismal
day. Doubts, excuses, and terror tumbled over one another as
they passed through my mind. It was too late to renege on
my story. They knew it was true. I fidgeted in my chair, then
folded and unfolded my hands.

"Cindy McCain."

Tim didn't react to my announcement, but Tom's head
jerked upright and he looked straight at me as if to challenge
me to repeat it.

My back straightened. "Cindy McCain. The Senator's
wife."

Out of the corner of my eye I saw Tim nod at Tom.

Was that my voice? Had I just identified the person I'd
been speaking about? My throat tightened until I thought

my breath would be cut off entirely. The agents sat silent. I still believed my friend had told his brother of the situation, but I wasn't certain of that. Tom, on the other hand, was obviously caught off guard by the name.

A flood of questions turned into a trickle and then dried up. After a brief summation of our meeting, they stood up to leave. As I closed the door behind them, I glanced at my watch. Only thirty minutes had passed—thirty minutes that would change my life forever.

As soon as the men had left and I'd put their glasses in the dishwasher, I sat down and wrote some notes about the meeting. Then I jotted down a few things I'd failed to mention and went to my room to reference the journal I'd been keeping for years. It held answers to the questions I wasn't able to address when I was asked.

Afterward, I sat down on the corner of my bed and contemplated the past hour. I felt like I'd dived from the side of a pool and was suspended in mid-air, not knowing if the water would be bathtub warm, icy cold, or somewhere in between. There'd been no mention of a follow-up meeting—only the assurance that they'd get back to me.

A few weeks passed before I heard from the agents, but they seemed eager to reconnect. After thorough investigation, they'd found the information I had provided to be accurate. The second meeting, less intimidating than the first and again at my apartment, consisted of more questions, many of which I answered on the spot. I promised to get back to them on the few I couldn't recall by saying I'd have to give the question some thought. I'd still not mentioned the journal or that I used it as a reference when I wasn't able to readily answer. The last thing I wanted to do was discredit myself by providing the agents with inaccurate information.

At the end of the second meeting, they told me they would investigate the new information and get back to me. The mood of this meeting had been even more relaxed, perhaps because they realized I wasn't some quack going after the McCains. Their commitment to pursuing the case seemed sincere, and I allowed myself to feel some relief, as well as reclaim a degree of confidence. We'd established a level of communication that bordered on camaraderie.

When we met the third time, I had my journal with me. It wasn't the fancy, leather variety, but rather a manila folder with two holes punched at the top and metal arms to hold the pages in place. It was organized from newest to oldest entries with the newest topping the stack. For the meeting, I'd put some markers in it so I could readily refer to my notes when answering questions regarding incidents I didn't fully recall.

The first time I referenced my journal, one of the agents said, "What is that?"

"It's my journal."

"What?"

"It's my professional journal. I started keeping it when I worked at America West. I attended so many meetings and met so many people I had to make notes to keep it all straight."

"Why are you referencing it now?"

"It has the answers to the questions you're asking."

I looked up at the agents. Their eyes reminded me of gluttons at a buffet.

"Do you want it?" I asked.

"Well, um, yeah."

"I'll make you a copy." Later, I learned that a contemporaneous journal—with all its grammatical errors—can be an important tool in any investigation.

As they read through the material, the agents discovered that Kathy provided most of the pertinent information contained in its pages. I'd not thought about it because it seemed that everyone in the office participated in the conversations about Cindy, but it was Kathy who shared most of the first-hand information. She had informed us about the various pharmacy invoices and also had mentioned a variety of doctors she thought might be involved.

My journal documented my observations, as well as the names and observations of other associated with AVMT. While I had no knowledge of how investigations proceed, I believed it provided the DEA agents with firsthand sources they could interview during their inquiry. Supporting this belief were numerous calls requesting clarification or asking me to expound on abbreviated notes.

One day when I was to meet the agents at the Coffee Plantation, the situation intensified. I arrived a few minutes early, got a coffee, and took a table outdoors. A few minutes later, Tim approached me and asked me to follow him. He took me to a sedan parked at the corner. After I'd taken a seat in the back and Tim had joined Tom in the front, they explained we were going for a ride so they could determine if I was being followed.

My heart pounded like a bass drum in my chest. Whenever I felt stressed, I reacted by distancing myself from the situation—as though I was an observer rather than a participant. Sounds and voices became faint and took on an echo-like quality, and I didn't speak. I focused on calming myself down. When I was confident I could talk normally, I asked for an explanation. The agents told me they'd confronted Cindy with some of their findings—which, of course, she'd denied. They believed she felt threatened by the confrontation, and they had concerns for my safety, as I was the most likely person that could have led them to those findings. After some forty-five minutes of driving through Tempe and south Phoenix, they took me back to my place. That day wasn't the usual question and answer session, nor did it infuse me with any confidence about the progression of the investigation. I'd never considered my safety to be an issue; but given their concerns, I had to consider that possibility. Both agents told me that should I ever feel uncomfortable or unsafe, I should contact them immediately.

From that time forward, I didn't feel at home in Phoenix and decided, once I'd seen the investigation to its conclusion, I would relocate. Meanwhile, I'd found temporary employment at Border's Book Store and had returned to America West to work in its America West Vacations Division. Although I had hoped to one day secure a position in some behind-the-scenes area of politics, I could no longer imagine working in a field where I would be crossing paths with the McCains. I feared my ill feelings would taint my ability to work amicably with them and hamper my effectiveness in any activity of which they were a part.

As the one year anniversary of my firing approached and the investigation into Cindy's alleged drug acquisition activities escalated, I began to contemplate a suit for wrongful termination. Arizona law required wrongful termination suits to be filed within a year of the termination date, so I'd sought the advice of a few people in the legal field. Although many of them thought I had a good case, they weren't willing to serve as my attorney because the firms they worked for either had ties to John McCain or the Hensleys—hence, a conflict of interest.

I began to lose hope that anyone would take my case.

## Chapter 15

I'd hoped the DEA's investigation of Cindy's illegal drug activities would be concluded prior to the anniversary of my firing. I thought that would help in a speedy settlement of my lawsuit. But because Cindy had been reluctant to accept responsibility for her wrongdoing, the investigation wasn't moving ahead.

I called Tim. "How much longer do you think it will take?"

"I don't know. Cindy doesn't realize we have a stack of evidence against her. We'll keep gathering information until that evidence is beyond question."

I paused to gather my thoughts. "Are a lot of drugs unaccounted for?"

"Based on the quantity of drugs that are missing and the frequency of the scripts, she may have been ingesting up to…uh…more pills than you can imagine anyone taking and still being able to function."

Tim's hesitation suggested he'd caught himself before he disclosed the specifics about the number of pills they calculated Cindy might have been taking. Based on what Kathy had told me about the quantities missing, either she consumed a large amount or she was stockpiling them for future use.

"Really? Would that explain why she drank so much milk?"

"Did she drink a lot of it?" Tim asked.

"Constantly. Directly from the carton."

"She may have needed it to settle her stomach. So many pills can raise hell with your gut."

I needed to get to the point of my call. "The one year anniversary of my termination is coming up, and I have to decide if I'm going to file a wrongful termination suit."

"I can't help you there. That's a separate issue," Tim said.

"I know. I just thought you should know it's coming up and that I'm considering it."

"I wish I could offer you some advice."

"Thanks."

I knew Tim wasn't in a position to offer me advice about any litigation I might pursue against Cindy, nor could he be specific about the status of the investigation. I'd just hoped he might say something that I could grasp as positive feedback during our conversation. Nothing I'd learned through the course of the investigation had led me to believe my hunches about Cindy's activities were wrong. Yet, with the DEA's work incomplete, I'd have neither documentation nor any person to back me up. It would be me against her—Tom Gosinski versus Cindy McCain—David confronting Goliath.

Finding an attorney to handle my lawsuit proved to be a daunting task. After eliminating those who had relationships with the McCains, the Hensleys, and the state's Republican party, I had few options left. I'd shared the details of Cindy's drug habit with only a handful of friends and family. In seeking counsel, I worried about disclosing too much information to anyone that I ultimately would choose not to work with. In fact, I was nervous about the whole situation—lawyers, DEA, the long-term ramifications of my involvement with Cindy during the period when she was using my name—along with others—to feed her habit. The last year had been so overwhelming that I'd begun to doubt my ability to recover from its devastating effects. All the insecurities I'd carried throughout my life began to surface, my lofty ideals about justice grew tarnished, and my confidence eroded along with my spirit.

Following the recommendation of several friends in the legal field, I contacted Stan Lubin, a Phoenix attorney known for his expertise in labor law and enthusiastic support of Democratic politicians. I wondered if the differences in our political philosophies would make it difficult for me to work with him. Given my situation, I decided that didn't matter.

With great trepidation I entered his office for our first meeting, but within minutes he put me at ease. We discussed my professional background, my job at the American Voluntary Medical Team, the circumstances regarding my termination, and my reason for wanting to file a suit. Stan asked who paid my salary, provided my benefits, and how AVMT was funded. I answered all the questions I could and committed to getting back to him with answers to the ones I couldn't.

Armed with what he learned from me, Stan drafted a demand letter to be sent to the McCains and a complaint that, should it be necessary, would be filed in court. The demand letter outlined Cindy's violations of my rights and the reasons I was entitled to relief. Stan also believed I had suffered retaliation in the form of my discharge because of my refusal to make false testament regarding the adoption of Bridget.

In reaction to the demand letter, John Dowd, the McCain's Washington, D.C., attorney, prepared a brief that was presented to the Maricopa County Attorney, suggesting the demand letter was a form of extortion. Yet, such letters are commonly sent in an attempt to settle cases prior to litigation.

On May 23, 1994, Terry Blake from the Maricopa County Attorney's office contacted me and advised me he had been asked to investigate my attempt to extort money from

Cindy McCain by suing her for wrongful termination. His inquiry, he said, would determine whether sufficient cause existed to move forward with the case.

"I thought the purpose of a demand letter was to attempt to settle cases prior to litigation, thus not burdening the courts," I said.

"Well—"

I didn't give him a chance to respond further. "How can it be extortion when I went to the DEA eleven months ago to tell them what I know?"

"You went to the DEA?" he asked.

"Yes. Eleven months ago. I've been cooperating in their investigation of Cindy for *eleven months*." I wanted to hammer the chronology of events into his head.

"Will you come in and talk to me?" Blake asked.

I agreed to meet with Mr. Blake at his office a few days later. Given the relationship I'd developed with the DEA's agents, I couldn't imagine talking to someone from the County Attorney's office would be difficult. I phoned Stan to inform him of Blake's call and the appointment I'd made to meet him.

"Don't go," Stan said.

"Why?"

"The County Attorney has the legal authority to *demand* your cooperation."

I hadn't considered that my cooperation in their investigation could strengthen their extortion case against me. What if I had met with them and misspoken? What if information I'd provided them was misinterpreted or misconstrued? Because of the comfortable and supportive relationship I'd developed with the DEA agents, I'd dropped my defenses and allowed myself to think cooperation with other agencies might not be damaging to me. I assumed everyone was working for a fair, judicial settlement of this situation, and I'd not allowed myself to imagine otherwise.

Contrary to my practice, I was a no-show at my appointment with Mr. Blake. I never heard from him or anyone from the County Attorney's office again. Regardless, Blake or someone in that office must have concluded that Dowd's charges had no merit because, without public announcement or the courtesy of advising me, the extortion investigation was closed. How did I find out? A local newspaper reporter informed me that there would be no charges against me—public information, it seemed.

Almost a year had passed since I'd gone to the DEA regarding my belief that Cindy was taking drugs from AVMT's inventory and that she might have used my name to obtain those drugs. I'd shared the dynamics of the organization's employees and that the office staff as a group had discussed her addiction and its potential consequences for all of us. Unfortunately for me, I doubted any of them would come to my defense because they were all still employees of AVMT and, I assumed, needed their jobs.

While Cindy knew the DEA was investigating the organization's drug records, whether she had informed her husband of it was an unknown. Keeping such a major investigation a secret would have had its challenges, but I wondered if she might try to muddle through it without involving him. Considering his apparent ignorance of her drug dependency, I perceived that as a possibility.

I marveled at the unbelievable situation I found myself in: I had a drug-addicted former boss whose absent husband—a U.S. Senator—might or might not be aware of his wife's abuse of prescription drugs. She was being investigated by the DEA—based at least in part on my report of missing drugs and unauthorized prescriptions at the non-profit medical services organization she headed up. The turn of events that had begun with my exit from America West Airlines to work for AVMT and ended with my dismissal flabbergasted me. Perhaps I knew too much about Cindy's drug use. To be sure, I had displayed an unacceptable penchant for telling the straight truth rather than adjusting it according to need.

With the deadline approaching and no time to lose, Stan filed the lawsuit. To his credit, he wrote it in general terms to make room for negotiation and to save the McCains from embarrassment. Neither of us wanted to publicly humiliate Cindy because we understood drug abuse to be an illness. I had mixed emotions about her and the situation she created, but I knew it would be difficult for her to find the help she required if her addiction was made public. Neither did I continue to view her as a friend, nor did I have any misconceptions that we'd ever mend our relationship. Still I was sympathetic because of the loneliness that I believed filled her life.

A local newspaper, the *Phoenix New Times*, discovered my suit in the county's court records and filed a Freedom of Information Act request for the details of the case. As a result, her secret life as a prescription drug addict exploded in the media. Because the DEA's investigation was ongoing, its files weren't public; the files generated by the extortion investigation were. Stan's discreet wording of my suit against Cindy had been to no avail. McCain's own attorney had exposed her addiction when he requested an extortion investigation. Otherwise, this information might never have been made public.

Somehow, the McCain camp learned of the *New Times* request for information. Prior to its release, they informed some McCain-friendly news organizations of Cindy's situation and made her available for interviews. The balance of the area's news organizations were forced to make reports based on information provided from the staged reports or "spin" provided by the McCains' lawyers and the public relations specialists they'd hired. Some reporters were sympathetic to her situation, and others were not.

Several of them contacted me. Although I refused to talk "on the record," I provided them questions they could ask others that I believed would lead them to the answers they desired. Upon reading their articles, however, I realized few of them had followed through on those leads because their stories were either chronologically incorrect or lacked any information beyond what had already been reported.

One reporter, Amy Silverman, of the *Phoenix New Times,* understood the misreporting that was taking place and proved she had a grasp of the true chronology. After several telephone conversations, I agreed to meet her in the paper's offices and provide the information she needed to write an accurate piece. For the most part, her article, "Opiate for the Mrs.," silenced the McCain camp's "spin" as it pointed out the inconsistencies in their information and accurately went through the chronology of events. Also, it made clear that I'd done nothing to make Cindy's addiction issues public, but in fact it was John Dowd's request for an extortion investigation that made it public record.

Eventually, my case against Cindy was dropped because of my inaction. I realized the cost of litigation would exceed the value of any judgment I might receive, so my pursuit of the case made no sense.

Months later, while I was in New York City to meet with a headhunter, my mom contacted me and said that Tim from the DEA office in Phoenix wanted me to call him. I'd not talked to Tim in a long time, so my curiosity got the best of me.

"Hey, Tim, it's Tom."

"How are you?" Tim asked.

"Mom told me you called."

"Where are you?" he asked.

"I'm in New York."

"Tom, we have something for you to show our appreciation for everything you did."

I envisioned a plaque for "Narc of the Year." I couldn't imagine where I'd hang it.

"Let me see what I can do. We can probably set up a meeting in our New York office."

"Great." I tried to sound excited, but I couldn't think of any award I could proudly display.

Tim got back to me with the specifics of the meeting. A few hours later, I arrived at the DEA's New York City headquarters in Manhattan. Upon entering, I was directed through a metal detector and then to a receptionist at the far side of the room. I stated my name and names of the agents Tim had told me to ask for. After a short wait, I was approached by two gentlemen in gray suits.

"Tom?" One man extended his hand and offered his name.

"Yes."

"Follow us."

We entered a conference room just off the lobby, and they gestured for me to sit down as they took seats on the opposite side of the table. One of them tossed a money bag in the center of the table.

"I'll count this into stacks of ten bills and then my partner will count them. If you'd like, you can also count them." As he spoke, the agent opened the bag.

"One hundred, two hundred, three hundred . . ." the counting went on until ten one-thousand-dollar stacks sat in front of me. Ten thousand dollars.

"What am I supposed to do with this?" I asked.

"We don't care. It's yours."

I was too stunned to speak. I had believed Tim was sending me to collect a piece of engraved wood.

"Here." One of them offered me the empty bag. "You can have this if you don't have anything to put it in."

Of course I'd not arrived prepared to depart with ten thousand dollars. "Is it safe to walk in this neighborhood with so much money?" I asked.

"You can catch a cab at the corner," one agent said.

"I don't know what you did, but it must've been a big deal," the other added as he stood to leave the room. "If you ever have anything for us, give us a call." They walked me to the front door and said their goodbyes.

"Tim. This is Tom. Thank you." I couldn't find words to express my appreciation.

"I hope it's enough. We'd like to have done more," Tim replied.

"I'd thought it might be a plaque or something." I laughed. "Thanks, Tim. Please tell Tom thank you, too."

I've never talked to Tim or Tom again. Their award meant much more to me than the dollar amount. It meant my cooperation in their investigation was both valuable and credible. Finally, I found a bright spot in the past dismal year.

## Chapter 16

Jump ahead to late summer, 2007.

After years of struggling with the notion that men should have jobs that required them to exercise their "business" or "management" minds, I acknowledged I was better suited to use the creative side of my brain. I'd always had an interest in interior and landscape design and possessed some natural talent in those areas, so I started providing design services to people in my hometown in Nebraska. Although I can't imagine ever growing rich by following my interest in design, I've realized satisfaction in creating interiors and landscapes that match people's lifestyles.

Originally, I returned home to help my mother care for my ailing grandmother but, following my grandmother's death, decided to stay in Nebraska and settle into a quieter life. That summer, the summer of 2007, I didn't feel overwhelmed by work, but I knew I was pushing my limits as I'd taken on large residential projects in Omaha and Denver and was criss-crossing Nebraska and Eastern Colorado to keep both jobs on schedule. Fortunately, I lived midway between the cities and could stop at home to rejuvenate, catch up on laundry, and mow the lawn. I spent much of the summer suffering from severe headaches, a self-diagnosed sinus infection, and fatigue. The lingering nature of the symptoms interfered with my lifestyle, and I took over-the-counter medications to minimize them.

It wasn't until a rather insensitive, matter-of-fact client told me I sounded tired that I sought medical help. My doctor, John, who is also my neighbor, squeezed me into his schedule and saw me as soon as I reached the office. He found no signs of an infection, nor could he give me any reason for my headaches; he referred me to an ear, nose, and throat specialist in Kearney, Nebraska.

On the day of the appointment, I didn't anticipate anything of significance because I'd not previously suffered from nose or ear problems. However, I did anticipate getting to Kearney and completing the appointment so I could do some shopping and go to lunch with my mom, who had made the trip with me in case I needed a relief driver. The ENT specialist, a pleasant young doctor, skillfully inserted a variety of stainless steel instruments into my nose and ears but, even with his training and experience, wasn't able to make a diagnosis. Without hesitation, he made an appointment for me to have an MRI and instructed me to go to the local hospital immediately. He also told me, once I'd completed the MRI, I was to return to his office to discuss its findings.

I still felt my situation was routine and the doctors were being thorough, especially since no one had said anything to cause alarm. This was my first MRI, and I was fascinated by the technology and the process. Even though I'd been told by others that the experience was unpleasant, I wasn't bothered by the noise or the claustrophobic environment created by the surrounding equipment.

I had a little time to waste after the unanticipated MRI, so my mother and I ate a quick lunch before returning to the ENT office. I wasn't able to see the doctor I'd met in the morning because he'd been called to surgery. Instead, I met with another young doctor who seemed hesitant to tell me the results. He explained that, from the examination the first doctor had done and the results of the MRI, I might have brain tumors. He'd already called a neurosurgeon and made an appointment for me to see him as soon as I could get to his office.

Although whatever was ailing me appeared to be a bit more serious than I had thought, I didn't experience any sense of alarm. Perhaps my brain wasn't allowing me to process the information—or my emotions were in defensive mode and didn't permit me to react.

My meeting with the neurosurgeon wasn't diagnostic, but rather an appointment to discuss the next step in the process. He informed me that I was to be at the hospital at six o'clock the following Monday morning for a stereotypic brain biopsy that would allow the doctor to remove small samples of brain tissue for testing. The surgery would require a halo to be put on my head so that it was stabilized. Then a drill would be used to put holes through my skull so samples could be removed. Also, an incision would be made in one of my temples, behind my hairline, where a larger sample would be taken.

Looking back now, I marvel at my calm objectivity. The physician's words rolled through my mind like a laundry list of to-dos. The explanation, the implication—all of it seemed almost anticlimactic after all I had gone through following my dismissal from AVMT. I had, for all practical purposes, begun my life over when I moved to Nebraska. Now it was being rearranged…again.

Unfortunately, my mother did not share my objectivity. The news hit her quite hard, and I could see her struggling to contain her fear for me. I was required to obtain a variety of documents—a living will and a resuscitation order—prior to the surgery because my life would be in jeopardy. (I still carried the opinion this would be a minor diagnostic procedure; apparently, no brain surgery is minor.) My friend, Scott Trusdale, completed the legal paperwork and brought it to the house for signature. Over the weekend, I mowed and worked in the yard, did some laundry, and contacted friends to inform them of my pending operation.

Mom and I drove to Kearney on Sunday night to avoid the fifty-mile trip early in the morning. We went to dinner and watched TV until both of us were ready to retire. At five o'clock Monday morning, she called my room to ensure I was up and getting showered so we could be at the hospital by five-forty-five for registration.

I don't recall much about the day. I was taken to a room where I put on a hospital gown and a variety of IVs were inserted into my arm. My next recollection was awakening in a hospital room. Mom and a nurse were present. Although drowsy, I felt surprisingly well. Afterward, I discovered small patches of hair had been shaved from my head, but I don't remember that happening.

I ate a small meal of bland food and gelatin and was allowed fluids, but otherwise I was encouraged to stay still. By late afternoon, I felt great and had even gone for a short walk. Except for the small scabs that had formed where the drill entered my skull and a few staples that closed the incision along my temple, everything seemed normal.

When my doctor did his rounds, I stated I was ready to leave the hospital. He told me he'd planned for me to wait until morning. However, because I was feeling well, he'd allow me to leave as soon as my dismissal paperwork could be processed. By eight o'clock that evening, I was lounging comfortably in my favorite chair.

Almost a week passed before I received a call that the neurosurgeon would like to see me to discuss the biopsy results. My severe headaches and the sensation I thought was a sinus infection, it turned out, were caused by toxoplasmosis, a brain parasite common in many people. It is most harmful to infants and those with compromised immune systems. The brain biopsy, in conjunction with my blood work, identified the severity of my illness—full-blown AIDS.

\* \* \* \* \*

It had been well over a decade since my trouble with Cindy McCain, yet she came to mind as the doctor's voice droned on about what I knew would be the greatest battle of my life. Eventually, she had faced the demon drugs that held her prisoner for years and moved on with her life. The Bangladesh baby she had adopted was a teenager heading into womanhood, she took over as chair of Hensley & Company after her father's death in 2000, and she continued to be involved in a number of philanthropic endeavors. It had been a rocky road, but she had survived. Suddenly, this woman who had been the source of so much grief in my life loomed in front of me, an example of overcoming the odds and living on for a better day.

The surgeon's voice pulled me back to the present. My mother was devastated by the thought that her son was gravely ill, and he gave her a comforting hug. I wasn't as interested in the moment as I was in the prognosis for the future. I've feared few things in life, and I wasn't about to let fear get in the way now. I wanted to know how to return to normalcy. The doctor talked about my blood work and the specifics of my diagnosis, but again I pushed his words aside. I didn't want to concern myself with the details or let statistics interfere with positive thinking. He'd already contacted the University of Nebraska Medical Center in Omaha and made an appointment for me to see an infectious disease specialist. That was all I needed to know. I wanted to get to Omaha and begin my journey to recovery.

"Are you old enough to drive?" My mom was giving the infectious disease doctor a critical look.

He smiled. "I am—I can even buy beer."

His youthful appearance and comforting manner invited questions. I felt immediately at ease with him. His youth impressed me because I believe young doctors who haven't been out of school for many years have the benefit of current knowledge and treatments. Like the doctors I'd seen previously, he went over my tests results. Although I acted interested, I didn't absorb any of the information. I'd had many friends who talked endlessly about their "numbers." I didn't want to be one of those people. I didn't want my life to be consumed by numbers and statistics because that seemed too similar to persons on a diet who weigh themselves daily—the results are never acceptable.

The doctor started me on a long list of drugs and made appointments for the future. In addition to getting the toxoplasmosis under control and alleviating the associated brain swelling—the cause of my headaches—he prescribed medication that would reverse the spiraling effects of AIDS.

My life soon consisted of doctors' appointments, MRI and CT scans, and a battery of drugs. By October the results from the drugs weren't sufficient, so I was admitted into the University of Nebraska Medical Center, where I was given stronger drugs to combat everything that was wrong in my body. After a ten-day stay at UNMC, I was released to go home with the understanding that my mom would give me twice-daily IVs and that I would be more or less bed-bound.

On December 3, I had a colonoscopy to detect whether something else might be interfering with my recovery. The next day, I received my first infusion of chemotherapy to combat Kaposi Sarcoma, an AIDS-related cancer that had formed in my colon. Since I wasn't ready to tell people the true results of the colonoscopy, I said I had "cancer in my colon" and hoped they wouldn't differentiate between my term and "colon cancer." That wording allowed me some time to deal with the realities of my situation.

Once the chemo started—I took treatments every twenty-one days—my health began to improve. By January I felt

I was getting better. Others disagreed. I suffered a few embarrassing falls, and at one point a doctor wanted to put me on hospice. I didn't see that as a viable alternative because I'd been burden enough for my mother. Given the hospice suggestion, however, I planned for the inevitable—my funeral. I arranged everything to relieve Mom of that terrible responsibility: music for the service, pall bearers, flowers, and even the reception. I never fancied myself a church-reception kind of guy, so I planned a party for the evening of the funeral. That seemed more Tom-like. Obviously, those plans were never executed, but I'm still happy they're in place.

By March I was driving myself to my chemotherapy appointments. I also adopted a dog, Honey, a Wheaten terrier from the Kearney Humane Society, and I was planning my forty-ninth birthday party. I know it's not common to celebrate one's forty-ninth, but given the circumstances, it seemed appropriate. My party took place in an Omaha hotel, and friends from as far as Los Angeles and New York City attended.

John McCain entered the 2008 presidential race that spring. Given his miserable performance in 2000 against George Bush, I didn't consider him a viable candidate. He had always played the POW card to his benefit; but his association with Charles Keating, Cindy's drug addiction issues, his lack of popularity within the Republican Party, his advanced age, and the walloping he suffered in 2000 made him an unlikely choice in my mind.

I could hardly contain my disbelief when he became the frontrunner in a party fractured by the Bush/Cheney administration. I couldn't imagine McCain uniting the GOP for a victory in 2008. Nonetheless, John's status as the presumptive general election candidate spawned press interest in Cindy's past addiction to pharmaceutical drugs—and in me.

My intention to avoid inquiries about my relationship with Cindy McCain and AVMT and instead to focus on my recovery didn't help me succeed in dodging the media. I received calls from the *Los Angeles Times, San Francisco Chronicle, Chicago Tribune, New York Times, Washington Post, Baltimore Sun, London Telegraph*, ABC, CBS, NPR, and a variety of online and freelance reporters. They all wanted me to expound on my years-earlier interview with Amy Silverman of the *Phoenix New Times*. Overwhelmed by the requests and afraid I'd mismanage the press, I continued my effort to limit exposure to them while handling their inquiries in an efficient manner.

To my surprise John Dowd, the McCains' legal pit bull, surfaced again. I had been told by a reporter that when he learned the *Washington Post* was investigating Cindy's past, he sent them letters questioning my character. Mr. Dowd had no knowledge of the physical challenges I'd endured, nor did he know my resolve. I'd faced a fearsome enemy and had survived. I certainly wasn't going to allow the McCains' lawyer to intimidate me at this late date.

In spite of his attempts to silence me, I went to Washington, D.C., met with a roomful of reporters, and answered all their questions. I also traveled to New York City, sat down for television interviews, and met with more reporters to address their inquiries. I never refused to answer a question, nor did my answers differ from those I'd offered years prior. I knew the facts of the situation, I was confident in them, and I relayed them honestly.

Once I'd met with reporters, I no longer viewed the McCains as a threat. Numerous articles have highlighted the discrepancies in their accounts of what happened. The reasons for her addictions and her treatments for those addictions changed from story to story, and I may never be convinced the truth has been told. Nor will I likely be persuaded that John McCain wasn't aware on some level of what was going on under his roof.

In the end . . . it doesn't really matter.

* * * * *

I may never be the person I was prior to encountering the McCains. I'd always lived by the motto: trust everyone until they give you reason not to. However, my trust in people and our institutions has been forever altered. I'll always question my ability to instinctively differentiate between people who are good and honest and those who aren't. I'll also find it difficult to trust our laws and the people charged with enforcing them; my experience has been that money talks louder than the law. What if Cindy McCain had been a poor, black or Hispanic mother from one of Phoenix's seedier neighborhoods who was caught stealing drugs from a pharmacy at which she worked? Would she have received the same treatment? Or would she have been subjected to a different standard?

Years earlier, Stan Lubin told me I was on *the wrong side of right.* I understood his inference and realized that, without money and/or power, sometimes it doesn't matter what side of *right* one is on. Today, with a greater understanding of Stan's words, I realize that being on the wrong side of Right isn't always a bad thing.

*Truth* will ultimately determine *Right.*

Writing this book has provided me an opportunity to tell my side of events that led to my dismissal from the American Voluntary Medical Team. Several others have shared their perspectives, and it's difficult for those who were not there to separate fact from fiction.

Unlike others, however, I see this as a story of two people and two diseases that redirected their lives. Cindy's addiction ruled her life during the time I worked for AVMT and dictated the way she treated people around her. I saw the pain it caused her, as well as the anguish it inflicted on those whose lives she touched. My AIDS diagnosis did not occur during the time I worked for Cindy, but it has had a profound impact on the way I view that period of my life. I have learned the gift of each day, greater appreciation for the beauty around me, and a better understanding of people's motives and the factors that drive them to do what they do. Compassion for circumstances never turns wrong into right, but it can foster comprehension, acceptance, and forgiveness.

Others may judge Cindy and me for our illnesses. Because of that, I empathize with her desire to hide the details of her disease—and her wish to escape the realities it thrust upon her—just as I chose for some years to keep my AIDS diagnosis private. Both Cindy and I know the personal truths of our respective afflictions, as well as what *really* happened that severed our relationship.

I now feel liberated from the silence that held me captive for so long. I hope—for Cindy, for me, and for all people—that someday we can live in a world that doesn't stigmatize certain illnesses and that we can all be relieved from the burden of keeping unnecessary secrets. Only then can we openly address rather than quietly bear our afflictions. Only then can we hope to avoid the suffering of living on the Wrong Side of Right.

# The Journal

**(Unedited)**

*This journal is just how it was when I presented it
to the Drug Enforcement Administration for
their investigation of Cindy McCain.*

*JULY 2, 1992*

*WHERE DO I BEGIN TO EXPLAIN THE OCCURRENCES OF JULY 2, 1992.*

*CARI MCCAIN, DAUGHTER OF JOHN AND CINDY MCCAIN, IS AT SCOTTSDALE MEMORIAL HOSPITAL WAITING TO HAVE HER APPENDICS REMOVED. ALTHOUGH SEVERAL PEOPLE (CARI, JERI JOHNSON, AND KATHY WALKER) TOLD CINDY THAT CARI HAD NOT FELT WELL AND HAD VISITED DOCTOR GOLDBERG ON THE PREVIOUS DAY, CINDY FAILED TO RECALL ANY OF THESE WARNINGS AND WENT BALLISTIC WHEN SHE WAS TOLD CARI WAS AT THE HOSPITAL AWAITING SURGERY.*

*SO, SHE TOLD JERI JOHNSON TO LEAVE THE HOSPITAL AND NOT TO RETURN.*

*WHAT A FAMILY. CINDY IS THE DAUGHTER OF JIM AND SMITTY HENSLEY, JERI JOHNSON IS SMITTY'S SISTER. CARI MCCAIN IS THE DAUGHTER OF JAMIE, JERI JOHNSON'S DAUGHTER. CINDY ADOPTED CARI FROM JAMIE AFTER JAMIE MOVED TO CALIFORNIA. CINDY AND JAMIE DO NOT SPEAK BECAUSE OF SOME FALLOUT WHICH OCCURRED SEVERAL YEARS AGO.*

*HAPPY NOTE - CARI HAD THE SURGERY AND IS DO-ING GREAT. HAPPIER NOTE - SHE STARTS COLLEGE IN AUGUST AND MAY HAVE AN OPPORTUNITY TO ESCAPE THE MADNESS.*

*JULY 3, 1992*

*WHAT A WAY TO START THE DAY. ON THE WAY TO WORK MY BEEPER WENT OFF - IT WAS CINDY, VERY UPSET, WANTING TO KNOW WHERE HER "FUCK-ING" VAN WAS. WHEN I STATED I DIDN'T KNOW, SHE TOLD ME TO FIND KATHY WALKER, AND MAKE SURE THE VAN WAS RETURNED TO HER THIS MORNING.*

*WELL . . . COME TO FIND OUT FRANK BRABED, WHO HAD BEEN WATCHING AFTER A SALVADORAN MOTHER AND SON AT THE MCCAIN HOUSE, HAD THE VAN. FRANK HAD BEEN GIVEN PERMISSION TO USE THE VAN BY JERI JOHNSON, CINDY'S AUNT AND A MEMBER OF THE AVMT STAFF.*

*CINDY CALLED TO APOLOGIZE. TOO LITTLE, TOO LATE. THE TONE FOR THE DAY HAD BEEN ESTAB-LISHED.*

*I CERTAINLY HOPE FOR ALL INVOLVED, AND MOST OF ALL, CINDY, THAT SOMEDAY IN THE NOT-TOO-DISTANT FUTURE A SENSE OF TRUST AND UNDER-STANDING WILL COME ABOUT. CINDY SEEMS TO BE DRIVEN BY SELFISHNESS AND A LACK OF TRUST FOR OTHERS. EVERYTHING IS BLOWN OUT OF PROPORTION AND IS ALWAYS BIGGER THAN LIFE.*

*JULY 8, 1992*

*SOME THINGS I MUST RECORD BEFORE I FORGET THEM:*

*THERESA THE NANNY. WHATEVER HAPPENED TO HER?*

*FLYING AIR FORCE ONE TO HAWAII FOR THE 50TH ANNIVERSARY OF    PEARL HARBOR. COULDN'T HAVE HAPPENED AS THE NEWS SAID THE PRESIDENT LEFT TWO DAYS AFTER JSM AND CHM.*

*ONLY CHILD. HOW ABOUT THE TWO HALF SIS-TERS? ONE IS JIM'S AND THE OTHER SMITTY'S.*

*CINDY HAS ASKED ME TO GIVE JIMMY SWIMMING LESSONS. I REALLY THINK JIMMY IS A GREAT KID SO I AGREED TO DO IT. I HAD REALLY THOUGHT IT WISE TO AVOID PARTICIPATION IN MCCAIN FAMILY PROJECTS BUT AS I AM SO INDEBTED TO CINDY I FEEL IT IS APPROPRIATE TO DO THIS. AGAIN, TIME WILL TELL IF MY DECISION IS A SOUND ONE. I HOPE SO.*

*WORKING ON THE UPCOMING MICRONESIA TRIP. DEPART ON THE 20TH FOR A QUICK ADVANCE - CINDY, KEN AND I. HOPE THE TRIP IS A GREATER SUCCESS THAN OUR RECENT TRIP TO EL SALVADOR. I REALLY FELT BAD ABOUT THE WAY WE TREATED THE VOLUNTEERS ON THAT TRIP. WE REALLY NEED TO TREAT THEM WITH MORE RESPECT AND ADMIRATION.*

*JULY 10, 1992*

*IT HAS BEN A PRETTY UNEVENTFUL TWO DAYS.
WORK HAS BEEN AVERAGE - WHICH AT AVMT
MEANS CHM HAS NOT CREATED ANY CRISIS.  HAVE
COMPLETED INPUTTING 2000 NAMES FOR A
FUNDRAISING LETTER WE WILL PRODUCE NEXT
WEEK - HOPE IT IS SUCCESSFUL AS THE ORGANI-
ZATION CAN CERTAINLY USE THE FUNDS.*

*TODAY I SENT A LETTER TO WASHINGTON TO
FIRM UP PLANS FOR OUR TRIP TO CHUUK, A
SMALL ISLAND IN MICRONESIA.  ALSO SPENT A
LITTLE TIME ORGANIZING A TRIP TO LOS ANGE-
LES TOMORROW EVENING TO TRANSPORT JOSE
AND MARIA RIVERA TO CONTINENTAL AIRLINES
SO THAT THEY MAY BEGIN THEIR JOURNEY HOME.
JOSE WAS BROUGHT TO PHOENIX FROM SAN SAL-
VADOR, EL SALVADOR TO RECEIVE TREATMENT
FOR CONGENITAL HEART DISEASE.  HIS SURGERY
AND RECOVERY WERE VERY SUCCESSFUL.  AFTER
TOMORROW NIGHT I WILL PROBABLY NEVER SEE
JOSE AGAIN BUT I AM SURE I WILL THINK OF HE
AND HIS MOTHER WHENEVER I HEAR MENTION
OF EL SALVADOR.*

*JULY 20, 1992*

*WELL IT HAS BEEN OVER A WEEK SINCE I LAST
MADE AN ENTRY TO MY JOURNAL.  A LOT HAS
HAPPENED.*

*LAST MONDAY I TRAVELED TO WINDOW ROCK,
ARIZONA TO MEET WITH THE NAVAJOS TO DIS-
CUSS A CONTRACT BETWEEN THE NAVAJO NATION*

*AND AVMT WHICH WOULD MAKE IT POSSIBLE FOR AVMT DOCTORS TO WORK ON THE RESERVATION WITHOUT FEAR OF MALPRACTICE SUIT.*

*SO I HAVEN'T HAD MUCH TO SAY ABOUT MRS. MC-CAIN. WELL, THIS MORNING I RECEIVED A CALL FROM FRANCIS FOTE, A DOCTOR WHO TRAVELED TO EL SALVADOR WITH AVMT. FOTE CALLED TO IN-FORM ME THAT HE HAD VISITED WITH CINDY ON FRIDAY REGARDING THE USE OF HIS DEA NUMBER. HE ASKED THAT I TELL CINDY HIS NUMBER COULD ONLY BE USED IN THE STATE OF NEW YORK AS THAT IS WHERE HE IS LICENSED. I DO NOT KNOW WHAT CINDY IS UP TO BUT IT APPEARS AS THOUGH SHE IS TRYING TO USE SEVERAL DOCTORS' DEA #'S SO THAT SHE CAN ACQUIRE DRUGS FOR PERSONAL USE. KATHY WALKER HAS STATED SEVERAL TIMES IN THE PAST THAT THIS HAS BEEN GOING ON FOR QUITE SOME TIME AND THAT THE DEA HAS QUES-TIONED LARGE ACQUISITIONS OF DRUGS SUCH AS PERCOCET. WE KNOW THAT 300 PERCOCET HAVE BEEN MISSING FROM AVMT'S INVENTORY AND THAT CINDY SAYS THEY ARE LOCKED UP AT HER HOME. I REALLY DON'T KNOW WHAT IS GOING ON BUT I CERTAINLY HOPE THAT CINDY DOES NOT GET HERSELF OR AVMT IN TROUBLE. I ALSO HOPE THAT IF IT IS NECESSARY, CINDY IS ABLE TO GET HELP BEFORE SHE DOES HERSELF HARM.*

*I HAVE DOCUMENTED WHAT I CAN REMEMBER OF THE PAST SEVERAL DAYS. I HOPE I DID NOT FORGET ANY SIGNIFICANT DETAILS. I HOPE THIS JOURNAL WILL BE FUN TO REFER TO IN THE FU-TURE AND IN THE PROCESS BE A HEALTHY EXER-CISE OF SELF EXAMINATION.*

*JULY 21, 1992*

*YESTERDAY PROVED TO BE A VERY LONG MONDAY. WE ARE BUSY INPUTTING A MAILING LIST INTO AVMT'S COMPUTER FOR AN UPCOMING FUND- RAISING LETTER. THE LIST WAS PROVIDED TO US BY JOHN MCCAIN'S CAMPAIGN OFFICE.*

*CINDY MCCAIN AND THE KIDS ARE AT THE FAMI- LY'S CABIN IN SEDONA. IT WOULD SEEM THAT IF THEY ARE OUT OF TOWN THINGS MIGHT SETTLE DOWN AROUND HERE BUT, IN FACT, THINGS BE- COME CRAZY AS SHE IS CONSTANTLY ON THE PHONE WITH US. CONSTANTLY IN THIS CONTEXT MIGHT BE DESCRIBED AS SEVERAL DOZEN PHONE CALLS PER DAY.*

*WHILE AT THE COFFEE PLANTATION, I RAN INTO THERESA WALHEIM, A FORMER NANNY OF THE MCCAINS. SHE WAS DISMISSED FROM THE MC- CAINS' SERVICE AFTER CINDY ALLEGED SHE HAD SEXUALLY MOLESTED THE MCCAINS' SEVEN YEAR OLD DAUGHTER, MEGHAN. I NEVER BE- LIEVED THAT THERESA WOULD COMMIT SUCH A CRIME AND HAVE SINCE THE TIME OF THE IN- CIDENT HEARD THAT NOT ONLY HAVE CHARGES BEEN DROPED BUT THAT THERESA PASSED A LIE DETECTOR'S TEST. CINDY, ON OCCASION, STILL MENTIONS THAT HER DAUGHTER WAS SEXUALLY ABUSED BY A FORMER NANNY. I WILL NEVER UN- DERSTAND THE REASONING BEHIND MANY OF CINDY'S ACTIONS. FOR THERESA I AM SURE THE INCIDENT WAS OVERWHELMING AS SHE IS A FOR- MER NUM AND THE ACCUSATION ITSELF WOULD CHALLENGE HER CREDIBILITY. FOR MEGHAN THE*

*FINAL STORY IS STILL OUT - SINCE THEN SEH HAS
ACCUSED HER ADOPTED SISTER, CARI (18 YEARS
OLD), OF GETTING UP DURING THE NIGHT AND
BEATING HER - WHAT A GRASP FOR ATTENTION.*

*JULY 22, 1992*

*WHAT A SLOW WEEK.*

*SINCE I HAD PLANNED TO BE IN MICRONESIA THIS
WEEK AND CINDY CANCELED TH TRIP AT THE
LAST MINUTE MY CALENDAR FOR THE WEEK IS
COMPLETELY OPEN. TRACY OFFICK AHD I HAVE
SPENT THE LAST THREE DAYS INPUTTING A NEW
FUNDRAISING LIST IN THE COMPUTER. IT IS NOT
FUN WORK BUT IT HAS TO BE COMPLETED.*

*WE HAVEN'T HEARD FROM CINDY TODAY - WHO
KNOWS WHAT SHE MIGHT BE UP TO. KATHY DID
FIND A DEA NUMBER FROM DOCTOR EVERTON ON
CINDY'S DESK THIS MORNING - I WONDER HOW
MANY OF THES NUMBERS SHE HAS GOTTEN AND
WHAT HER PURPOSE IS. TO DATE, TRACY, KATHY
AND I KNOW THAT ON FRIDAY OF LAST WEEK
SHE REQUESTED DEA NUMBERS FROM DRS. TOM
MOFFO, FRANCIS FOTE, KELLY REBER, MAX JOHN-
SON, DE LA PAVA AND EVERTON. I CERTAINLY
HOPE THAT SHE DOES NOT GET ALL OF THESE
GUYS IN A LOT OF TROUBLE.*

*JULY 23, 1992*

*WE HAVEN'T HEARD FROM CINDY TODAY. YES-
TERDAY I FOUND OUT SHE HAD A MEETING
WITH KEN AKERS, AVMT'S PHOTOGRAPHER. I AM*

*A LITTLE UPSET THAT I WAS NOT TOLD ABOUT
THAT MEETING AS LAST WEEK I HAD A MEETING
WITH KEN TO DISCUSS CUTTING HIS DAILY RATE
IN HALF - FROM $500 TO $250 - CINDY HAS ASKD
ME TO DO THIS AS A COST SAVING MEASURE. I AM
ANXIOUS TO FIND OUT THE RESULTS OF SHE AND
KEN'S MEETING.*

*JULY 24, 1992*

*THIS MORNING I APPEARED IN JUVENILE COURT
TO TESTIFY ON BEHALF OF NICKI GULLETT, THE
BABY WE BROUGHT BACK FROM BANGLADESH
AND WHO IS NOW BEING ADOPTED BY WES AND
PAM GULLETT. IT WAS MY FIRST TIME TO BE
SWORN IN - KIND OF A NICE FEELING TO KNOW
THAT THIS LITTLE GIRL IS GOING TO HAVE A
MUCH BETTER LIFE THAN SHE WOULD HAVE HAD
IN BANGLADESH.*

*I FINISHED INPUTTING MY LIST OF NAMES INTO
THE COMPUTER FOR OUR UPCOMING FUNDRAIS-
ING LETTER. SMALL HURDLES ARE GREAT TO
PASS.*

*TRACY ORRICK HAS BEEN A REAL BITCH TODAY.
THIS MORNING WHEN I CALLED THE OFFICE
COLLECT FROM A PAY PHONE IS MESA SHE HUNG
UP BEFORE SHE EVEN LISTENED TO THE MESSAGE.
I WAS VERY SHORT WITH HER AND TOLD HER
NEVER TO HANG UP ON SOMEONE AGAIN - GOD
KNOWS WHAT WOULD HAVE HAPPENED HAD
THAT BEEN CINDY. WHEN I ARRIVED BACK IN
THE OFFICE SHE BLASTED ME IN FROM OF JANET
VACEK, A FORMER AVMT EMPLOYEE, FOR BEING*

*SHORT WITH HER ON THE PHONE. I PULLED HER INTO MY OFFICE AND TOLD HER THAT HAD I SPOKEN TO CINDY THAT WAY I WOULD EXPECT TO BE FIRED - I TOLD HER I WOULD NOT TOLERATE ANOTHER SUCH INCIDENT. IT DOESN'T PAY TO BE EASY ON PEOPLE - SHE HAS GOTTEN A LITTLE TOO CONFIDENT OF HERSELF.*

*JULY 27, 1992*

*WHAT AN INTERESTING MONDAY.*

*JERI JOHNSON RETURNED FROM A WEEK'S STAY IN LA JOLLA WITH ALL KINDS OF NEWS REGARDING CHM.*

*IT SEEMS CHM HAS DECIDED O BUY THE HOME NEXT TO HER CURRENT HOME IN SEDONA TO EXPAND THEIR PROPERTY THERE. JIM HENSLEY, HER FATHER, HAS AGREED WITH THE BUY AND WILL SUPPORT CINDY'S DECISION.*

*JERI SAID THAT WHILE SHE WAS IN LA JOLLA A GREAT MANY CONVERSATIONS TOOK PLACE REGARDING CHM'S POSSIBLE DRUG USE. CINDY'S PARENTS ARE NOW BOTH AWARE OF THE PROBLEM AND JERI SAYS ARE PREPARED TO CONFRONT CINDY WITH THE ISSUE. JERI SAID THAT CARI CLARK MCCAIN HAS VOICED CONCERNS FOR THE CHILDREN AND THAT DIANE, ONE OF THE NANNIS, HAS ASKED TO MEET WITH HER TO DISCUSS "PROBLEMS". I THINK THAT EVERYONE INVOLVED HAS NOTICED THE EXTREME MOOD SWINGS WHICH OCCUR AT RELATIVELY SMALL TIME INTERVALS.*

*I HAVE ALWAYS WONDERED WHY JOHN MCCAIN HAS DONE NOTHER TO FIX THE PROBLEM. HE MUST EITHER NOT SEE THAT A PROBLEM EXISTS OF DOES NOT CHOOSE TO DO ANYTHING ABOUT IT. IT WOULD SEEM THAT IT WOULD BE IN EVERY-ONE'S BEST INTEREST TO COME TO TERMS WITH THE SITUATION AND DO WHATEVER IS NECESSARY TO FIX IT. THERE IS SO MUCH AS RISK: THE WEL-FARE OF THE CHILDREN; JOHN'S POLITICAL CA-REER; THE INTEGRITY OF HENSLEY & COMPANY; THE WELFARE OF JIM AND SMITTY HENSLEY; AND THE HEALTH AND HAPPINESS OF CINDY MCCAIN.*

*THE AFOREMENTIONED MATTERS ARE OF GREAT CONCERN TO THOSE DIRECTLY INVOLVED BUT MY MAIN CONCERN IS THE ABILITY OF AVMT TO SURVIVE A MAJOR SHAKE-UP. IF THE DEA WERE TO CONDUCT AN AUDIT OF AVMT'S INVENTORY I AM AFRAID OF WHAT THE RESULTS MIGHT BE. FROM WHAT JERI JOHNSON AND KATHY WALKER HAVE TOLD ME CHM HAS, FOR QUITE SOME TIME, BEEN TAKING FROM AVMT'S INVENTORY TO SAT-ISFY THE NEEDS OF HER ADDICTION. BOTH HAVE TOLD ME THAT VOLUMES OF PERCOCET HAVE BEEN FOUND MISSING AND THAT CINDY ALWAYS PROVIDED THEM WITH FLIMSY ACCOUNTINGS OF THE DRUGS WHEREABOUTS. IT IS BECAUSE OF CHM'S WILLINGNESS TO JEOPARDIZE THE CRED-IBILITY OF THOSE THAT WORK FOR HER THAT I TRULY WORRY.*

*DURING MY SHORT TENURE AT AVMT I HAVE BEEN SURROUNDED BY WHAT ON THE SURFACE APPEARS TO BE THE ULTIMATE ALL AMERICAN FAMILY. IN REALITY, I AM WORKING FOR A VERY*

*SAD, LONELY WOMAN WHOSE MARRIAGE OF CON-*
*VENIENCE TO A U.S. SENATOR HAS DRIVER HER*
*TO : DISTANCE HERSELF FROM FRIENDS; COVER*
*FEELINGS OF DESPAIR WITH DRUGS; AND REPLACE*
*LONELY MOMENTS WITH SELF-INDULGENCES.*

*JULY 28, 1992*

*CINDY AND I ARE TRAVELING TO THE EAST COAST*
*NEXT WEEK. WE ARE GOING TO WDC AND POSSI-*
*BLY NEW YORK TO MEET WITH REPRESENTATIVES*
*OF PHARMACEUTICAL COMPANIES TO DISCUSS*
*DONATIONS OF DRUGS AND SUPPLIES TO AVMT.*
*I AM HOPING THAT THE TRIP WILL BE SUCCESS-*
*FUL - NOT ONLY IN ACQUIRING THE DRUGS THE*
*ORGANIZATION NEEDS BUT ALSO IN ACTING AS*
*A MEANS OF MOTIVATING CHM'S INTEREST IN*
*AVMT.*

*JERI JOHNSON SAID THAT SHE MET WITH DIANE,*
*CINDY'S NANNY, LAST NIGHT. DIANE VOICED*
*CONCERNS REGARDING CINDY'S USE OF DRUGS*
*AND THE EFFECT IT IS HAVING ON THE KIDS. DI-*
*ANE TOLE JER THAT MEGHAN RECENTLY TOLD*
*HER TO "FUCK OFF" AFTER TRYING TO DISCIPLINE*
*HER. SHE ALSO TOLD JERI THAT SHE IS CON-*
*CERNED CINDY IS GIVING THE KIDS DRUGS THAT*
*UNNECESSARILY SEDATE THEM. I HOPE THAT*
*THAT IS NOT HAPPENING.*

*JULY 29, 1992*

*THE FUNDS WE HAVE RECEIVED OFF OF THE*
*MOST RECENT FUNDRAISING LETTER ARE COM-*
*ING IN RATHER SLOW. IN THE LAST THREE DAYS*

*WE HAVE RECEIVED $570. ALTHOUGH THIS
AMOUNT DOES NOT BEGIN TO COVER OUR DAILY
EXPENSES IT DOES PROVIDE US WITH A DONOR
LIST WHICH WE CAN WORK AT A LATER DATE. I
WOULD REALLY LIKE TO SEE OUR FUNDRAISING
TAKE OFF BUT IT IS VER HARD TO DO WITHOUT
CINDY'S INVOLVEMENT AND COOPERATION.*

*JERI JOHNSON SAID THAT JIM AND SMITTY ARE
GOING TO CONFRONT CINDY ABOUT HER DRUG
PROBLEM. I DON'T KNOW WHAT THE END RESULT
WILL BE BUT I FEAT THAT IT MAY BE THE END OF
A AVMT AND MY JOB. SHOULD AVMT BE CLOSED
DOWN, I TRUST JIM HENSLEY WILL TAKE CARE OF
ALL OF US UNTIL WE ARE ABLE TO FIND OTHER
MEANS OF INCOME. I HAVE TO HAVE NASTY
THOUGHTS , BUT THIS FAMILY CANNOT AFFORT
TO HAVE ANY OF US LEAVE THIS ORGANIZATION
WITH NEGATIVE FEELINGS. WE ALL KNOW TOO
MUCH ABOUT THE WAS CINDY AND JOHN CON-
DUCT THEIR PERSON LIVES. NOT A PRETTY PIC-
TURE.*

*JULY 31, 1992*

*CINDY AND I ARE TO SPEND MOST OF NEXT WEEK
BETWEEN WASHINGTON AND NEW YORK. I HOPE
THAT OUR TRIP IS A SUCCESSFUL ONE - AVMT
NEEDS A GOOD SHOT IN THE ARM.*

*MISS JERI CONTINUES TO TELL MCCAIN STORIES.
JERI TOLD US THAT LAST NIGHT WHEN SHE,
CARI MCAIN, AND HIM AND SMITTY HENSLEY
HAD DINNER CARI INFORMED ALL OF THEM
THAT CINDY HAS A VERY BAD DRUG PROBLEM.*

*CARI STATED THAT HER MOODS SWING FROM
ANIMATED HIGHS TO DARK LOWS. CARI FEELS
THAT CINDY DOES NOT LIKE HER AND IS ANXIOUS
FOR HER TO LEAVE. CARI TOLD THE THREE THAT
SHE FEARS CINDY GIVES THE KIDS PRESCRIPTION
DRUGS THEY DO NOT NEED. SHE ALSO TOLD
THE GROUP THAT CARL AND JERI PETERSON
ARE AWARE OF THE PROBLEM AS IS DENNIS,
THE SEDONA CARETAKER. JERI SAID THAT
SMITTY INTENDS TO DEAL WITH ISSUE UPON
HER RETURN FROM THEIR TRIP TO EUROPE - IN
THE MEANTIME HIM ASKED CARI TO OBTAIN A
SAMPLING OF THE PILLS CINDY IS TAKING.*

*AUGUST 3, 1992*

*THINGS ARE PRETTY QUIET IN THE OFFICE TO-
DAY - CINDY AND I DEPART FOR A BUSINESS TRIP
TO WDC AND NEW YORK AT 11:15 PM. I AM STILL
WAITING FOR JOHN MCCAIN'S OFFICE TO FAX US
THE WEEK'S ITINERARY. HOPE IT COMES SOON AS
I KNOW CIND WILL BE CALLING TO ASK WHAT OUR
SCHEDULE IS.*

*AUGUST 7, 1992*

*ON MONDAY NIGHT AT 9:50 CINDY CALLED TO
INFORM ME THAT MEGHAN WAS HAVING A TAN-
TRUM ABOUT HER DEPARTURE FOR WDC AND
NEW YORK. CINDY BLAMED THE OUTBURST ON
MEGHAN'S FEAR OF WHAT MIGHT OCCUR IN HER
MOTHER'S ABSENCE - A REPEAT OF THE ALLEGED
SEXUAL MOLESTATION BY THERESA, THE FAMILY'S
FORMER NANNY, OF MEGHAN DURING CINDY'S
TRIP TO VIETNAM. ALL OF US WHO ARE FAMILIAR*

*WITH THE INCIDENT NOW KNOW THAT THERESA DID NOT MOLEST MEGHAN NOR WAS MEGHAN MISTREATED IN ANY WAY. THE ENTIRE STORY WAS A CHM FABRICATION WHICH BROUGHT A GREAT AMOUNT OF PAIN TO ALL INVOLVED AND WHICH, I FEAR, IS GOING TO HAVE A NEGATIVE IMPACE ON MEGHAN IN THE FUTURE. NEEDLESS TO SAY, I WAS TOLD TO TAKE THE DELTA AIRLINES RED EYE TO WDC BY MYSELF AND CONDUCT THE MEETINGS SCHEDULED FOR CINDY. THE MEETINGS WHICH I ATTENDED WENT FINE, HOWEVER, AS THE MEETINGS WERE SCHEDULED FOR MRS MCCAIN I AM POSITIVE THE HOSTS WERE DISAPPOINTED BY HER ABSENCE.*

*CINDY AND MEGHAN ARRIVED IN WASHINGTON ON TUESDAY NIGHT. CINDY CONTINUED THE STORY OF MEGHAN'S PROBLEMS STEMMING FROM THE THERESA INCIDENT. I DIDN'T SPEND MUCH TIME VISITING WITH CINDY AS ALL OF US WERE TIRED AND THE FOLLOWING DAY PROMISED TO BE LONG.*

*WEDNESDAY CONSISTED OF TWO MEETING WITH PHARMACEUTICAL COMPANIES, A VISIT TO JAY SMITH'S OFFICE (JAY SMITH IS ONE OF JOHN MCCAIN'S CAMPAIGN CONSULTANTS) AND A FUNDRAISER FOR JOHN AT THE RONALD REAGAN CENTER. THE FUNDRAISER FEATURED PJ O'ROURKE A POLITICAL SATIRIST AND WAS ATTENDED BY SEVERAL PROMINENT SENATORS AND CONGRESSMEN: PHIL GRAHAM, JOHN WARNER, KOLBY, RHODES AND STUMP. I HAD A NICE CONVERSATION WITH O'ROURKE - WE BOTH WERE IN VIETNAM AND BANGLADESH DURING THE LAST YEAR AT APPROXIMATELY THE SAME TIME.*

*THURSDAY CINDY AND I WITH MEGHAN IN TOW TRAVELED TO NEW JERSEY TO VISIT MORE PHAR-MACEUTICAL COMPANIES - BECTOM & DICKIN-SON AND JOHNSON & JOHNSON. BOTH MEET-INGS WENT RELATIVELY WELL EVEN THOUGH CINDY TOLD SOME MISTRUTHS. WHILE VISITING WITH B&D CINDY STATED THAT AVMT PARTICI-PATED IN RELIEF FOLLOWING THE SAN FRANCIS-CO EARTHQUAKE. NOT!!*

*WHILE TRAVELING BY LIMO TO JFK CINDY WAS CONTACTED BY KATHY WALKER AND WAS TOLD THAT THE BOYS, JACK AND JIMMY, HAD BEEN PLAYING AND TAKEN SOME MEDICINE. COME TO FIND OUT THAT IN FACT THE BOYS HAD ONLY BEEN MIXING A "POTION" AND HAD NOT TAKEN ANY OF THE DRUGS. I WAS AMAZED BY REACTION - SHE IMMEDIATELY FEAR THE WORST (MAYBE SHE FEARED THE BOYS HAD DISCOVERED HER STASH OF PAIN PILLS) AND WHEN SHE FOUND OUT, NOT THAT THE BOYS WERE OUT OF DANGER BUT THAT THEY HAD BEEN PLAYING WITH "NON STASH" DRUGS, SHE ALMOST IMMEDIATELY DISMISSED THE ISSUE AND, IN FACT, MADE LIGHT OF IT.*

*AUGUST 10, 1992*

*WORK IS THE SAME. CHM IS IN PHOENIX TODAY AND, AS IS COMMON THESE DAYS, IS UP TO HER OLD TRICKS. SHE TOLD KATHY THIS MORNING THAT SHE HAS A CALL IN TO DR MOFFO. I CER-TAINLY HOPE SHE DOESN'T GET HIM TO WRITE PRESCRIPTIONS FOR PAIN PILLS. ALSO, WE RE-CEIVED A BILL THIS MORNING FROM PROFES-SIONAL PHARMACY FOR VICODIN AND APAP WITH*

*CODEINE, 200 UNITS EACH, THE PRESCRIPTION WRITTEN BY MAX JOHNSON. I CANNOT BELIEVE THE AMOUNT OF DOCTORS WHO KNOWINGLY CONTINUE TO FILL HER PRESCRIPTIONS.*

*AUGUST 11, 1992*

*WORKING AT AVMT CONTINUES TO GIVE ME REA- SON TO LAUGH. YESTERDAY CINDY CALLED TO TELL KATHY AND I TO WEAR OUR RED AND KHAKI CLOTHING AS SH WANTED AVMT TO APPEAR TO BE A GRASS ROOTS OPERATION FOR THE ATTORNEYS WHO ARE TO PERFORM A DEPOSITION REGARDING MAX JOHNSON'S SUIT WITH HIS INSURANCE COM- PANY. IMAGINE, US DRESSED IN AVMT ATTIRE WORKING IN THE HENSLEY & CO BUILDING - ONE OF THE NICEST PRIVATELY OWNED OFFICE FACILI- TIES IN THE CITY. ANYWAY, KATHY AND I SHOWED UP IN OUR AVMT STUFF TODAY - CINDY ARRIVED IN HER SCRUBS - I DON'T KNOW IF WE LOOK LIKE GRAS ROOTS ORGANIZERS OR CLOWNS BUT AS HAS BEEN THE CASE IN RECENT PAST, I AM DOING EX- ACTLY WHAT TH BOSS ORDERED.*

*SINCE CINDY IS IN THE OFFICE TODAY I AM SURE TOMORROW'S ENTRY WILL BE INTERESTING.*

*AUGUST 14, 1992*

*WORK STARTED OFF AT A RELATIVELY NORMAL PACE THIS MORNING. AND THEN KATHY RECEIVED A CALL FROM ROYAL NORMAN AT CH 3 REGARD- ING A POSSIBLE AVMT TRIP TO SOMALIA. BEFORE KATHY INFORMED ME OF HER CONVERSATION WITH ROYAL SHE TOLD CINDY AND CINDY JUMPED*

*ALL OVER THE ISSUE. NOW CINDY WANTS TO AIR-
LIFT A LOAD OF SUPPLIES TO SOMALIA AND USE
CH 3 TO GET THE COVERAGE SHE SO DESPERATELY
GOES AFTER. I THINK THE WHOLE IDEA IS CRAZY
AS WE HAVE SO MUCH TO DO WITH THE NAVAJOS
BUT CINDY SEEMS INTENT ON MAKING IT HAPPEN.*

*KATHY ASKED CINDY ABOUT THE BILL FOR THE
DRUGS I REFERRED TO IN MY 10AUG92 ENTRY AS
KATHY HAS NOT RECEIVED THEM FOR INVENTORY
FOR AVMT. CINDY TOLD KATHY THAT THOSE
DRUGS AND SOME ANTIBIOTICS WERE SENT TO
MICRONESIA WITH MILITARY PERSONNEL SINCE
AVMT WAS UNABLE TO MAKE A TRIP TO THAT AREA
THIS YEAR. TO THE BEST OF MY KNOWLEDGE NO
DRUGS OR SUPPLIES OF ANY KIND WERE SENT TO
MICRONESIA.*

*I AM BECOMING VERY CONCERNED ABOUT THE
AMOUNT AND MEANS BY WHICH CINDY IS OBTAIN-
ING DRUGS. ALTHOUGH I DO NOT KNOW WHAT
CINDY'S INTENDED USE OF THE DRUGS IS NOT DO
I KNOW EXACTLY WHERE THE DRUGS ARE BEING
STORED I CAN ONLY ASSUME THAT CINDY IS OB-
TAINING THESE DRUGS FOR HER PERSONAL CON-
SUMPTION. I CERTAINLY HOPE THAT CINDY DOES
NOT RISK HER HEALTH OF THE HEALTH OF HER
CHILDREN IN HER PURSUIT OF THIS ADDICTION.
AUGUST 14, 1992*

*WELL CINDY HAS DONE IT AGAIN. JERI PETERSON
FROM THE HOUSE CALLED TO INFORM KATHY
THAT ANOTHER BATCH OF DRUGS WERE PICKED
UP AT THE PHARMACY TODAY AND THAT KATHY'S
NAME IS ON THE BOTTLES. DR. TOM MOFFO*

*PRESCRIBED THE DRUGS FOR CINDY - KATHY WOULD NOT KNOW OF THE TRANSACTION HAD JERI PETERSON NOT TOLD HER.*

*IT IS BECOMING MORE AND MORE DIFFICULT NOT TO SAY SOMETHING REGARDING THIS IS-SUE, HOWEVER, THE BIG QUESTION IS, TO WHOM SHOULD SOMETHING BE SAID. CINDY'S PARENTS HAVE ALREADY BEEN INFORMED ABOUT HER DRUG PROBLEM, JOHN MCCAIN HAS KNOWN ABOUT IT FOR SOME TIME, THE ENTIRE HOUSE STAFF IS AWARE, AND BOB DELGADO HAS LET IT BE KNOWN HE IS NOT INTERESTED IN BEING IN-VOLVED WITH SUCH MATTERS.*

*MY CONCERN IS NO LONGER FOR CINDY BUT FOR ALL OF THE OTHER INDIVIDUALS WHO COULD BE RUINED SHOULD THE TRUTH BE KNOWN. GOD KNOWS SHE IS NOT GOING TO GO DOWN WITH-OUT TAKING SOME OF THEM WITH HER. WITH MATTERS SUCH AS THIS IT IS ONLY A MATTER OF TIME BEFORE THE WHOLE THING EXPLODES - I HOPE IT DOES NOT EXPLODE IN MY FACE.*

*ALTHOUGH KNOWLEDGE IS OFTEN CONSIDERED TO BE POWER, I WOULD PREFER THAT I KNEW NOTHING OF CINDY'S ADDICTIONS AS I FEAR THE END RESULT.*

*AUGUST 18, 1992*

*CINDY AND JOHN ARE IN HOUSTON THIS WEEK FOR THE REPUBLICAN NATIONAL CONVENTION. CINDY CALLED ON SUNDAY NIGHT TO LET ME KNOW THAT THEY WOULD BE TRAVELING FROM*

*INDIANAPOLIS TO HOUSTON ON AIR FORCE ONE
AS THEY AND THE BUSHES ARE ATTENDING A
VFW CONVENTION IN INDIANAPOLIS ON SUNDAY
NIGHT. WHAT AN EXCITING LIFE JOHN AND CIN-
DY LEAD.*

*AUGUST 21, 1992 - FRIDAY*

*CINDY AND JOHN RETURNED FROM THE REPUBLI-
CAN CONVENTION TODAY. JOHN'S SPEECH LAST
NIGHT WAS FULL OF WORTHY MESSAGES BUT HIS
DELIVERY WAS LESS THAN INSPIRATIONAL. CINDY
SOUNDED AS THOUGH SHE HAD A GOOD TIME AT
THE CONVENTION. I INQUIRED WHAT THE PRES-
IDENT'S INTENTIONS WERE FOR JOHN AND SHE
STATED THAT, OFF THE RECORD, THE PRESIDENT
MAY ASK JOHN TO SERVE AS SECRETARY OF DE-
FENSE. EVERYTHING IS CONTINGENT UPON THE
OUTCOME OF BOTH THE PRESIDENT'S AND JOHN'S
CAMPAIGNS - JOHN BEING NAMED AS SECRETARY
OF DEFENSE MIGHT MEAN THAT I WOULD HAVE
AN OPPORTUNITY TO MOVE TO WASHINGTON.*

*AUGUST 25, 1992 - TUESDAY*

*WHAT A CRAZY 24 HOUR PERIOD. SINCE I MADE
MY ENTRY YESTERDAY WE, AVMT, HAS BEEN
CALLED UPON TO PROVIDE ASSISTANCE TO MIAMI
AND NEW ORLEANS DUE TO THE EXTREME DAM-
AGE BOTH AREAS INCURRED DUE TO HURRICANE
ANDREW. SO FAR WE HAVE BEEN ABLE TO COOR-
DINATE THE TRANSPORTATION OF BABY PROD-
UCTS AND FOOD TO THE MIAMI AREA AND MOBI-
LIZATION OF EMT PERSONNEL FROM SOUTHWEST
AMBULANCE TO NEW ORLEANS. I HAVE A FEELING*

*THAT BEORE THIS MATTER IS PUT TO REST THE EMT PERSONNEL MAY BE SENT TO MIAMI WHERE THE NEED SEEMS TO BE MUCH GREATER THAN IN THE NEW ORLEANS AREA.*

*AT THE SAME TIME WE ARE PREPARING FOR A TRIP TO NORTHERN KENYA TO ASSIS SOMALIAN REFUGEES WHO ARE AT GREAT RISK BECAUSE OF A SHORTAGE OF FOOD SUPPLIES. SEVERAL HUN-DRED THOUSAND SOMALIANS ARE REPORTED TO BE AR RISK - A WAR IN THEIR HOME COUNTRY HAS MADE RELIEF EFFORTS IMPOSSIBLE. WE HOPE TO DEPART FOR SOMALIA ON OR ABOUT THE 8TH OF SEPTEMBER AND RETURN ON ABOUT THE 16TH. CINDY, MAX JOHNSON, KEN AKERS AND I WILL BE ACCOMPANIES BY A SKELETON TEAM OF DOCTORS AND NURSES TO DELIVER SUPPLIES WE ARE ABLE TO ACQUIRE AND TO PROVIDE MINIMAL CARE TO THE NEEDY PEOPLE.*

*ANYWAY, THINGS ARE STILL CRAZY AT AVMT; CINDY IS BACK IN HER 20 PHONE CALLS PER DAY MODE - NO SINGLE CALL BEING WORTH THE EN-ERGY SPENT TO DIAL OR ANSWER. IF CINDY WERE EVER ABLE TO IMPROVE ANY ASPECT OF HER MAN-AGEMENT ENERGIES - SO MUCH OF OUR TIME IS SPENT ON THE PHONES, CLARIFYING INSTRUC-TION, AND COVERING OUR ASSES I AM SURPRISED ANY WORK IS ACCOMPLISHED. OH WEL, SHE SIGNS THE CHECKS.*

*AUGUST 28, 1992*

*WORK HAS BEEN CRAZY - CINDY DECIDED WE SHOULD TAKE A LOAD OF SUPPLIES TO THE*

*MIAMI AREA TO ASSIST IN THE HURRICANE ANDREW RELIEF EFFORTS. IT WOULD BE SIMPLE TO COMPLETE THE TASK IF CINDY WOULD NOT INTERFERE WITH THE REST OF US DOING OUR JOBS, HOWEVER, SHE IS CONSTANTLY STIRRING THINGS UP.*

*WE ARE ALSO CONTEMPLATING A TRIP TO SOMALIA - MARK SALTER IN JOHN MCCAIN'S WASHINGTON OFFICE HAS STATED THAT THE STATE DEPARTMENT AND THE DEPARTMENT OF DEFENSE BELIEVE IT IS NOT SAFE TO TRAVEL TO SOMALIA OR THE NORTHERN REGIONS OF KENYA. CINDY INSISTS THAT WE ARE GOING TO GO ON THE TRIP AND THAT IT MAY BE WISE FOR US TO PACK GUNS.*

*SHE IS ABSOLUTELY CRAZY - I DON'T KNOW HOW TO LOAD A GUN LET ALONE SHOOT ONE.*

*I FEEL REALLY BAD THAT CINDY IS SO DEPENDENT UPON THE DRUGS THAT SHE TAKES - NOT SO MUCH FOR HER AS HER FAMILY AND ALL OF THE PEOPLE THAT WORK FOR HER. HER MOOD SWINGS ARE VERY UNPREDICTABLE AND EVERYONE IS FEARFUL OF THE ACTIONS SHE MIGHT TAKE SHOULD HER MOOD BE BAD. IT IS DIFFICULT TO WORK IN FEAR OF A WOMAN DEPENDENT ON DRUGS.*

*I AM OFF TO FLORIDA ON SUNDAY WITH A SHIPMENT OF SUPPLIES, BACK LATE MONDAY NIGHT AND OFF TO NEW YORK TO VISIT WITH STEVE REINER AT PRIME TIME AND HOPEFULLY MAKE SOME INITIAL CONTACTS FOR MY NEW YORK JOB SEARCH.*

*SEPTEMBER 2, 1992 - WEDNESDAY*

*TODAY IS A PERFECT EXAMPLE OF WHY SOMEONE SHOULD WAIT TO VENT THEIR FRUSTRATIONS - SPONTANEOUS COMBUSTION CAN BE DANGEROUS.*

*THIS PAST WEEK AT AVMT HAS CERTAINLY BEEN A CHALLENGE. ALL OF US THAT WORK FOR CINDY HAVE BEEN ASKED TO PUT IN EXTENDED HOURS AT NIGHT AND ON THE WEEKEND AND HAVE NOT RECEIVED A THANK YOU. CINDY IS THE MOST DEMANDING AND THANKLESS PERSON I HAVE EVER MET.*

*LAST FRIDAY, KATHY, TRACY AND I HELPED SECURE, BOX AND PLACE ON PALLETS 19774 LBS OF CARGO TO BE SHIPPED TO MIAMI FOR HURRICANE ANDREW RELIEF. BEYOND THAT I SOLICITED FREE TRANSPORTATION OF THE FREIGHT WITH AMERICA WEST AND UPS AND FREE AIRLINE TICKETS FOR MYSELF, KEN AKERS AND STEVE TORBECK. FOR THAT I RECEIVED NO THANKS.*

*SUNDAY WE TRAVELED TO ORLANDO WITH CINDY. THE ENTIRE WEEKEND WAS INSINCERE MEETINGS, PHOTO OPS FOR JOHN MCCAIN'S UPCOMING ELECTION AND PLANNING FOR FUTURE OPPORTUNITIES. CINDY EVEN LIED ABOUT BEING INVITED BY THE PRESIDENT TO PARTICIPATE IN A MOTORCADE OF THE DEVASTATED AREA - SHE WAS IN FACE INVITED BY A STAFFER PRIOR TO THE BUSHES' ARRIVAL AT HOMESTEAD - THE PRESIDENT AND MRS BUSH DIDN'T EVEN KNOW CINDY WAS IN FLORIDA UNTIL AF1 LANDED AT HOMESTEAD.*

*TODAY WE WERE INFORMED THAT AVMT WOULD RETURN TO MIAMI NEXT WEEK WITH A CONSTRUCTION TEAM - CINDY DECIDED THAT THE MALPRACTICE ISSUE WAS TOO BIG TO DEAL WITH. TO DATE WE HAVE NO MATERIALS TO TRANSPORT TO THE AREA FOR OUR WORK AND CINDY HAS NOT MADE ANY OF THE CALLS SHE SAID SHE WOULD TO SOLICIT THE SUPPLIES.*

*ABOUT CINDY'S DRUG PROBLEM - TODAY KATHY ASKED CINDY ABOUT THE INVOICE FOR DRUGS PRESCRIBED BY TOM MOFFO, THE SECOND SUCH PRESCRIPTION IN TWO WEEKS. CINDY STATED THE DRUGS HAD BEEN SENT TO TWO DIFFERENT ISLANDS IN THE FEDERATED STATES OF MICRONESIA WITH A NAVY OFFICER AND THAT I HAD BEEN AWARE OF THE REQUEST AND AVMT'S RESPONSE. WHEN KATHY TOLD ME ABOUT CINDY'S STATEMENT I CALLED CINDY TO INQUIRE ABOUT THESE TWO SHIPMENTS ABOUT WHICH I HAVE NO KNOWLEDGE AND CINDY CHANGED THE STORY AND SAID THAT KATHY WAS CONFUSED AND THAT WHAT ACTUALLY HAPPENED WAS THAT THE SHIPMENT HAD IN FACT BEEN SENT WITH THE NAVY OFFICER BUT IT HAD BEN SO SMALL THAT SHE HAD SIMPLY HAD HIM PUT IT IN HIS LUGGAGE - SHE STATED THE SHIPMENT WAS "PENICILLIN AND A FEW ITEMS DR MOFFO HAD PUT TOGETHER FOR HER."*

*MY TRIP TO NEW YORK WAS CANCELED FOR TODAY AT THE LAST MOMENT. I WAS TO HAVE DINNER WITH STEVE REINER OF ABC'S PRIME TIME. UNFORTUNATELY, SINCE I WORK FOR A CRAZY, DRUGGED WOMAN NO PLANS ARE EVER SURE UNTIL THEY HAVE BEEN EXECUTED. I HOPE THAT*

*I GET OUT OF THIS ENTIRE MESS SOON - I DO NO
T FEEL GOOD ABOUT MY CURRENT JOB, I HAVE
A GREAT AMOUNT OF ANIMOSITY FOR MY BOSS,
AND AM EXERTING A GREAT AMOUNT OF STRESS
RELATED ENERGY THINKING BAD THINGS ABOUT
AVMT AND CINDY HENSLEY MCCAIN.*

*SEPTEMBER 3, 1992 - THURSDAY*

*THIS JOURNAL IS BECOMING MORE LIKE A BITCH
PAD THAT THE DIARY OF MY DAILY LIFE I HAD IN-
TENDED IT TO BE.*

*WORK IS CRAZY AS USUAL. THE TRIP TO FLORIDA
ON MONDAY IS ON SCHEDULE - WE ARE NOW
TRAVELING AS A CLEAN UP CREW IN BLUE HOS-
PITAL SCRUBS. I QUESTIONED WEARING SCRUBS
BUT CINDY INSISTED THAT THE "VISUAL" IS IM-
PORTANT, SO . . . WE ARE GOING TO RUMMAGE
THROUGH THE RUBBLE OF HURRICANE ADREW IN
SCRUBS.*

*WHATEVER . . .*

*PER MRS MCCAIN THE AVMT SCHEDULE FOR
THE NEXT COUPLE OF WEEKS IS AS FOLLOWS;
MIAMI CLEANUP FROM SEPTEMBER 7 THROUGH
SEPTEMBER 11; NAVAJO NATION PARADE
SEPTEMBER 12; AND DEPART FOR SOMALIA ON
SEPTEMBER 13. CINDY MUST THINK THAT WE
HAVE A STAFF OF 20 AS SHE HAS CERTAINLY
NOT SAT DOWN, LOOKED AT A CALENDAR AND
RATIONALLY THOUGHT ABOUT WHAT SHE IS
SUGGESTING WE ACCOMPLISH.*

*OVER THE PAST FEW WEEKS I HAVE GROWN TO HAVE A GREAT DISTASTED FOR POLITICS AND THE POLITICAL SYSTEM. I HAVE NEVER BEEN SO AWARE OF THE AMOUNT OF INSINCERITY BEHIND A POLITICAL CAMPAIGN AS I AN NOW WITH JOHN MCCAIN'S REELECTION CAMPAIGN. EVERYTHING CINDY MCCAIN DOES IS POLITICALLY MOTIVATED AND DRIVEN BY THE ALMIGHTY "PHOTO OP". I AM CONVINCED THAT CINDY MCCAIN COULD GIVE A RAT'S ASS ABOUT THE CITIZENS OF THIRD WORLD COUNTRIES OF THE VICTIMS OF NATURAL DISASTERS. IF CINDY WAS A COMPASSIONATE PERSON IT WOULD BE REFLECTED IN THE WAY SHE CONDUCTS HERSELF DAY-TO-DAY, HOWEVER, THAT SIMPLY IS NOT THE CASE. CINDY IS PROBABLY THE MOST INSECURE, SELFISH, THANKLESS SELF-SERVING INDIVIDUAL I HAVE EVER MET.*

*JERI JOHNSON BUSIED HERSELF THE PAST COUPLE OF DAYS COLLECTING INVOICES OF PRESCRIPTIONS PURCHASED BY CINDY TO SUPPORT HER ADDICTION TO PAIN PILLS. I KNOW THAT SHE HAS PHOTOCOPIED A BILL FOR DRUGS PRESCRIBED BY DOCTOR MOFFO AND FILLED AT PROFESSIONAL PHARMACY. JERI HAS ALSO STATED THAT JIM HENSLEY HAS ASKED THAT SHE OBTAIN FROM TOM HOLTRIP (AVMT'S, HENSLEYS' AND THE MCCAINS' BOOKKEEPER) PHOTOCOPIES OF PAST BILLS FROM PHARMACIES FOR DRUGS ORDERED BY CINDY, SUPPOSEDLY, ONCE ENOUGH INFORMATION HAS BEEN PILED, JIMMY HENSLEY IS GOING TO CONFRONT CINDY WITH FACTS ABOUT HER HABIT. I'LL BELIEVE IT WHEN I SEE IT.*

*SEPTEMBER 4, 1992*

*THINGS SEEM TO HAVE SETTLED DOWN A BIT - EITHER CINDY HAS INCREASED HER PERCOCET INTAKE OF SHE IS BUSY THINKING ABOUT OTHER THINGS.*

*THE TRIP TO FLORIDA FOR MONDAY IS COMING AROUND. WE ARE GOING TO DO A CLEAN UP IN THE HOMESTEAD AND FLORIDA CITY AREAS. WE ARE TAKING A MINIMUM SUPPLY OF TOOLS AND ARE STAYING IN A FL LAUDERDALE HOTEL SO THE LOGISTICS OF THIS TRIP ARE RELATIVELY EASY.*

*SEPTEMBER 14, 1992*

*WELL I'M BACK AT MY DESK AFTER A WEEK OF TRAVELING WITH MRS MCCAIN AND AVMT TO SOUTHERN FLORIDA TO HELP IN THE RELIEF EF-FORTS FOLLOWING HURRICANE ANDREW. WHAT A WEEK!*

*THE TRIP WAS, FOR ALL PRACTICAL PURPOSES, A SUCCESS. I BELIEVE THAT HAD CINDY GIVEN ME THE OPPORTUNITY TO ORGANIZE OUR EFFORTS WE WOULD HAVE REALIZED GREATER ACCOM-PLISHMENTS BUT I ALSO UNDERSTAND THAT A LOT OF WHAT WE DO IS DONE FOT THE SOLE PUR-POSE OF "PHOTO OPPORTUNITY".*

*CINDY SPENT MOST OF HER TIME WITH KEN AK-ERS, AVMT PHOTOGRAPHER, AND DID NOT DIS-PLAY ANY DESIRE TO SPEND MUCH TIME WITH TH REST OF THE GROUP NURTURING RELATIONSHIPS. AS A LEADER, CINDY DOES NOT TRY TO INSPIRE*

*OTHERS TO BE TEAM PLAYERS BY PRESENTING AN
IMAGE OF COMRADAERIE.*

*I DID NOT WITNESS ANY EXTREME MOOD SWINGS
IN CINDY THIS TRIP. ON WEDNESDAY EVENING
TRACY AND I OBSERVED A SLIGHT CHANGE
IN HER MOOD AND ALSO NOTICED THAT SHE
WOULD NOT MAKE EYE CONTACT. SHE SEEMED A
BIT REMOVED AND SAID SHE HAD A LOT OF WORK
TO DO. HOWEVER, AS SOON AS KEN RETURNED
FROM AN ERRAND IN MIAMI SHE WAS AS GREGARI-
OUS AS ANYONE IN THE GROUP. MAYBE SHE JUST
DOESN'T LIKE US AND WANTED TO SPEND TIME
WITH KEN.*

*ON FRIDAY CINDY CALLED ME FROM PHOENIX TO
INFORM ME THAT I SHOULD PREPARE THE TEAM
TO TRAVEL TO KAUI, A HAWAIIAN ISLAND, TO AS-
SIST WITH THE VICTIMS OF HURRICANE INIKI. I
DON'T THINK SHE THINKS ENOUGH OF OTHER
PEOPLE TO EVER SAY THAY YOU OR RECOGNIZE
THEIR CONTRIBUTIONS TO THE ORGANIZATION
BUT I WAS IN NO MOOD FOR THESE ORDERS SINCE
I HAD NOT YET COMPLETED OUR MIAMI MISSION
AND HAD NOT HAD MY WORK ACKNOWLEDGED. I
WOULD FEAT I AM BEING OVER SENSITIVE WAS IT
NOT FOR THE FACT THAT OTHER PEOPLE I WORK
WITH HAVE ALSO VOICE SIMILAR SENTIMENT.*

*SINCE OUR RETURN, JERI JOHNSON INFORMED
ME THAT CINDY'S PARENTS ARE GOING TO CON-
FRONT HER REGARDING HER DRUG PROBLEM
UPON THEIR RETURN FROM THE CHRISTENING
OF THE USS MCCAIN IN MAINE. THEY ARE SUP-
POSEDLY GOING TO DEMAND A DRUG TEST ON*

*MONDAY THE 28TH AND DEPENDING ON THE OUTCOME OF THAT TEST WILL THEN FORCE HER ENTRY INTO A TREATMENT FACILITY. ALSO, TRA-CY ORRICK TOLD ME THAT KATHY WALKER WAS INFORMED TODAY OF YET ANOTHER BATCH OF DRUGS ORDERED IN KATHY'S NAME.*

*I HOPE THAT CINDY'S ABUSIVE NATURE DOES NOT CAUSE THE DOWNFALL OF A HOST OF GOOD PEOPLE.*

*SEPTEMBER 15, 1992 - TUESDAY*

*WORK IS GOING VERY SLOWLY TODAY. I WAS ABLE TO SOLICIT 10 ROUND TRIP TICKETS ON AMERICA WEST AIRLINES AND ALOHA AIRLINES FOR TRAVEL TO KAUAI TO ASSIST THE VICTIMS OF HURRICANE INIKI. I DON'T KINOW IF THE DONATIONS WILL BE USED AS CINDY HAS NOT MENTIONED THE TRIP SINCE HER INITIAL TELEPHONE CALL LAST FRIDAY. REGARDLESS, I HAVE DONE WHAT WAS ASKED OF ME - OBTAINING FREE ROUND TRIP AIR FAR FOR THE AMERICAN VOLUNTARY MEDICAL TEAM.*

*SEPTEMBER 16, 1992 - WEDNESDAY*

*NOT A WHOLE LOT OF NEWS - RELATIVELY SLOW DAY IN PARADISE.*

*WORK IS QUIET TODAY. AS USUAL I DISCOVERED A FEW MORE LIES CINDY HAS TOLD US OVER THE PAST COUPLE OF DAYS:*

*CINDY HAS BEEN SICK SINCE MONDAY AFTER-NOON. SHE INITIALLY BLAMED HER ILLNESS ON*

*FOOD THAT SHE TOLD US CARL PETERSON HAD PICKED UP FOR LUNCH. TODAY CARL TOLD US HE DIDN'T PICK UP LUNCH ON MONDAY.*

*YESTERDAY I TOLD CINDY I HAD OBTAINED 10 FREE ROUND TRIP SEATS FROM AMERICA WEST AND ALOHA AIRLINES FOR AVMT'S TRIP TO KUAIA. CINDY SAID SHE HAD DISCUSSED THE MISSION WITH MARK SALTER OF JOHN MCCAIN'S WASHINGTON OFFICE AND HAD NOT YET RECEIVED INFORMATION SHE HAD REQUESTED BACK FROM HIM. TODAY, I VERY CASUALLY ASKED MARK IF HE KNOW OF OUR INTENTIONS TO TRAVEL TO KUAIA AND HE STATED HE KNEW NOTHING ABOUT IT.*

*I TRULY DO NOT UNDERSTAND WHAT MOTIVATES (OR TROUBLES) CINDY TO TELL SO MANY LIES. I AM SURE IT HAS EVERYTHING TO DO WITH BEING VERY UNHAPPY. HER MARRIAGE SUCKS. HER LIFE HAS BECOME A CONFUSED MESS BECAUSE OF RESOURCES - MONEY, STAFF, CLOUT. AND SHE HAS BURNT SO MANY BRIDGES SHE HAS NO ONE TO CONFIDE IN OR LOOK TO FOR SUPPORT. I FEEL VERY SORRY FOR TH UNHAPPINESS CINDY IS OBVIOUSLY EXPERIENCING, HOWEVER, THE UNHAPPINESS SHE INFLICTS ON OTHERS IS UNFORGIVABLE.*

*SEPTEMBER 18, 1992 - FRIDAY*

*WELL IT IS WEEK'S END. THIS WEEK HAS BEEN ONE OF TH LEAST I HAVE EXPERIENCED IN QUITE SOME TIME. I SPENT MONDAY AND TUESDAY, OR AT LEAST A PORTION OF EACH OF THOSE DAYS WORKING ON AN AVMT TRIP TO KAUAI ONLY TO HAVE CINDY DECIDE SHE DIDN'T WANT TO GO. I*

*OBTAINED FREE ROUNDTRIP TRANSPORTATION FOR 10 THROUGH AMERICA WEST AIRLINE AND ALOHA AIRLINES. INSTEAD OF TELLING ME SHE JUST DIDN'T WANT TO GO CINDY HAD TO MAKE UP A LIE AND TELL ME SHE HAD VISITED WITH SENATOR INOUYE'S OFFICE AND WAS TOLD THAT OUR ASSISTANCE WAS NOT NEEDED. OH WELL.*

*SEPTEMBER 21, 1992 - MONDAY*

*I DIDN'T HEAR FROM CHM THIS WEEKEND - I RE-ALLY NEEDED A VACATION FROM THE PHONE CALLS AND PAGING. I SOMETIMES COME DOWN ON HER PRETTY HARD IN THIS DOCUMENT - GEN-ERALLY I BELIEVE IT IS JUSTIFIED - BUT I BELIEVE MOST OF HER PROBLEMS STEM FROM LONELI-NESS AND UNHAPPINESS. I HOPE FOR HER THAT SOMEONE HAS THE COURAGE TO CONFRONT HER ABOUT HER DEPENDENCY PROBLEM AND CAN HELP HER TO FIND HAPPINESS. SHE HAS THE PO-TENTIAL TO BE A GREAT PERSON - SHE HAS THE MENTAL CAPACITY, RESOURCES AND WHIT RE-QUIRED TO DO GREAT THINGS.*

*SEPTEMBER 23, 1992 - WEDNESDAY*

*I RECEIVED NEWS THIS MORNING THAT THE NA-VAJO NATION SIGNED A RESOLUTION ALLOWING THE AMERICAN VOLUNTARY MEDICAL TEAM TO WORK ON THE NATION. THE AGREEMENT ALLOWS AVMT TO WORK ON THE NAVAJO NATION FREE OF EXPOSURE TO MALPRACTICE SUIT. I AM ANXIOUS TO READ THE FINAL DOCUMENT WHICH IS TO BE FAXED TO ME TODAY.*

*WE ARE HAVING A STAFF MEETING NEXT WEDNES-*
*DAY - IT WILL BE OUR FIRST ORGANIZED MEET-*
*ING IN MONTHS. I ASKED CINDY IF WE SHOULD*
*PREPARE ANYTHING FOR THE MEETING AND SHE*
*STATED NO. SO . . .*

*SEPTEMBER 24, 1992*

*WORK IS VERY QUIET. CINDY HEAD BACK EAST*
*FOR THE CHRISTENING OF THE USS JOHN S MC-*
*CAIN, A NEW DESTROYER NAMED AFTER JOHN'S*
*FATHER. THE DEDICATION IS TAKING PLACE IN*
*BATH, MAINE. AS IS USUAL, CINDY HAS MADE A*
*HUGE PRODUCTION OF THE EVENT.*

*NEWS FLASH! CINDY AND HER ADOPTED DAUGH-*
*TER, CARI, HAVE NOT BEEN GETTING ALONG VERY*
*WELL, SO . . . CINDY DECIDED NOT TO TAKE CARI*
*TO THE SHIP CHRISTENING AND HAD HER NOTI-*
*FIED BY KATHY, CINDY'S SECRETARY. SHE IS REAL-*
*LY A WITCH - WHAT MOTHER COULD BE SO CRUEL*
*AS TO NOT INCLUDE HER DAUGHTER IN SUCH*
*AN EVENT. I NEVER CEASE TO BE AMAZED BY THE*
*LEVEL OF DISREGARD AND OUTWARD HATRED*
*CINDY SHOWS FOR SO MANY PEOPLE.*

*I HAVE BEEN REALLY UNEASY FOR THE*
*LAST SEVERAL DAYS WITH THE WAS AVMT IS*
*PROGRESSING. JERI JOHNSON TELLS ME THAT*
*THE ORGANIZATION'S DAYS ARE NUMBERED BUT*
*THAT I MAY BE IN LINE FOR A POSITION WITH*
*HENSLEY & CO. AT THE SAME TIME, CINDY IS*
*SO FAR OFF BALANCE THESE DAYS THAT I DON'T*
*KNOW FROM MOMENT TO MOMENT IF I AM*
*IN OR OUT. WORKING UNDER SUCH STRAINED*

*CONDITIONS HAS CERTAINLY BEEN FRUSTRATING AND I WILL, AT THE EARLIEST OPPORTUNITY, QUIT THIS POSITION TO TAKE ANOTHER.*

*SEPTEMBER 28, 1992 - MONDAY*

*ALL OF US AT AVMT ARE ON PINS AND NEEDLES WAITING TO HEAR ABOUT THE OUTCOME OF JIM AND SMITTY'S CONFRONTATION WITH CINDY. WE HAVE BEEN TOLD BY JERI JOHNSON THAT THE CONFRONTATION WILL OCCUR EITHER TODAY OR TOMORROW AND SINCE WE ARE NOT SURE OF WHAT CINDY'S REACTION WILL BE WE FIND IT VERY DIFFICULT TO GO ABOUT OUR DAILY DUTIES. I HOPE THE WHOLE ORDEAL MOTIVATES US ALL TO MOVE ON GOD KNOWS, IF I WASN'T DEPENDENT ON THE INCOME I WOULD HAVE TAKEN OFF A LONG TIME AGO. LESSON: NEVER PUT YOURSELF IN A POSITION WHERE YOU ARE IN-DEBTED TO AN EMPLOYER OR WORK ASSOCIATE.*

*SEPTEMBER 29, 1992 - TUESDAY*
*THE NEWS AT AVMT CONTINUES TO CENTER AROUND CINDY MCCAIN'S DRUG DEPENDENCY PROBLEM. CINDY'S PARENTS, JIM AND SMITTY HENSLEY, WERE TO CONFRONT CINDY ABOUT HER PROBLEM EITHER YESTERDAY OR TODAY AND NOT IT APPEARS THEY MAY BE GOING THROUGH THEIR OWN STATE OF DENIAL. AFTER HAVING OBSERVED CINDY AT THE CHRISTENING OF THE JOHN S MCCAIN IN BATH, MAINE, THE HENSLEYS FEEL CINDY IS ACTING PERFECTLY NORMAL.*

*JERI PETERSON, CINDY'S HEAD HOUSEKEEPER, TRAVELED TO MAINE WITH THE FAMILY TO WATCH*

*AFTER THE KIDS. SHE HAS TOLD JERI JOHNSON THAT CINDY BEHAVED LIKE A CAGED ANIMAL WHILE IN MAINE AND THAT SHE HAS NEVER BEEN SO BAD. I FEAR WHAT WILL HAPPEN IF SOMETHING IS NOT DONE ABOUT CINDY IN THE VERY NEAR FUTURE. SHE HAS CERTAINLY MADE ALL OF THOSE WHO WORK FOR HER MISERABLE AND IT IS SCARY TO THINK WHAT SHE MIGHT DO IF SHE BECOMES EVEN LESS COHERENT AS TO HOW NORMAL PEOPLE CONDUCT THEIR LIVES.*

*REGARDLESS OF WHAT HAPPENS WITH CINDY MC-CAIN, IT IS TIME FOR ME TO GET OUT OF AVMT. I HAVE SO LITTLE RESPECT FOR CINDY AND HER OBJECTIVES - SHE HAS MADE AVME A MEDIA EVENT - THAT EVEN UNDER THE BEST OF CIRCUMSTANCES I DO NOT THINK THIS ORGANIZATION MERITS EXISTENCE. IF IT WERE NOT FOR MY DEPENDENCY AND NED FOR INCOME I WOULD LEAVE THIS ORGANIZATION WITHOUT THE SECURITY OF HAVING FOUND A NEW JOB.*

*I GUESS WHAT DISGUSTS ME MOST IS MY INABILITY TO HAVE SEEN THROUGH THE SMOKE SCREEN, BEING TAKEN IN BY THE GLAMOUR. BEYOND THAT I FEEL AS THOUGH I AM NOT BEING A RESPONSIBLE HUMAN BECAUSE I CONTINUE TO WATCH A WOMAN WITH A GREAT AMOUNT OF POTENTIAL SLIDE DEEPER AND DEEPER INTO A DEPENDENCY WHICH CONTROLS HER - A WOMAN WHO HAS FOCUSED ALL OF HER ENERGIES AT SURVIVING IN A DARK, WARPED WORLD.*

*AND THE UNATTENDED RESPONSIBILITIES GO ON AND ON: THE DOCTORS WHO HAVE INNOCENTLY*

*PRESCRIBED DRUGS FOR CINDY BELIEVING THEY WERE TO GO INTO AVMT'S INVENTORY; THE LONG TERM SCARS WHICH ARE BEING INFLICTED ON THE MCCAIN CHILDREN; THE UNHAPPINESS BEING EXPERIENCED BY THE STAFF AT AVMT; AND THE PAIN THE HENSLEYS MUST BE EXPERIENCING AT AN AGE WHEN LIFE SHOULD BE ONLY PLEASURE.*

*WELL, I CAN HOLD MYSELF ACCOUNTABLE FOR ALL OF THESE PROBLEMS OR I CAN ERASE THEM FROM MY CONSCIENCE - I HOPE I CAN DEAL WITH MY CONCLUDING DECISION.*

*SEPTEMBER 30, 1992 - WEDNESDAY*

*WELL, WHAT A MORNING. THE STAFF MEETING THAT HAD BEEN SCHEDULED FOR 1100 WAS MOVED TO 0900. THOSE IN ATTENDANCE: CINDY MCCAIN, BOB DELGADO, TRACY ORRICK, KATHY WALKER AND MYSELF. JERI JOHNSON WAS NOT INCLUDED IN THE MEETING.*

*CINDY CONDUCTED THE MEETING AND DISCUSSED SEVERAL POINTS. THE FIRST TOPIC WAS TEAM WORK. CINDY STATED THAT SHE HAD BEEN INFORMED BY PEOPLE BOTH INSIDE AND OUTSIDE THE ORGANIZATION THAT THE AVMT STAFF WAS NOT WORKING AS A TEAM. SHE SAID WE MUST WORK TOGETHER TO REACH THE ORGANIZATION'S OBJECTIVES AND HAT SHE WOULD NOT TOLERATE ANY OTHER CONDUCT. SECONDLY, CINDY STATED THAT ON SEVERAL DIFFERENT OCCASIONS SHE HAD BEEN TOLD THAT PEOPLE HEARD FROM INSIDE THE ORGANIZATION THAT AVMT WAS*

*BEING USED FOR POLITICAL POSTURING AND THAT SHE INTENDED TO DUMP IT ONCE JOHN'S REELECTION CAMPAIGN WAS CONCLUDED. I CAN'T IMAGINE WHO IN THIS ORGANIZATION WOULD SAY SUCH THINGS AD I ALSO CAN'T IMAGINE WHO WOULD CONFRONT CINDY WITH SUCH ISSUES AT A SOCIAL OR POLITICAL EVENT. CINDY ALSO STATED THAT REGARDLESS OF WHAT WE ALL THINK OF KEN AKERS HE WILL CONTINUE TO WORK FOR THE TEAM, THAT KEN HAS LONG BEEN A FRIEND OF THE MCCAINS AND THAT THE RELATIONSHIP WILL NOT BE TERMINATED.*

*ON A PERSONAL LEVEL CINDY COMPLIMENTED TRACY ON HER WORK, SUGGESTED TO KATHEY THAT SHE BECOME MORE INVOLVED WITH THE VENDORS FROM WHOM SHE HAS OBTAINED SUPPLIES, AND TOLD ME THAT I NEED TO SPEND MORE TIME ON THE ROAD DOING FUNDRAISING.*

*BEYOND THE MEAT OF THE MEETING, CINDY STATED THAT: SHE SPENDS A LOT OF TIME AT NIGHT AND ON THE WEEKEND DOING WORK IN THE OFFICES - HER HOURS; AS STAFF WE SHOULD NOT ALIENATE PROSPECTIVE TEAM MEMBERS BY ACTING ALOOF; AND THAT SHE IS THE BOSS, THERE IS NO PECKING ORDER AND THAT AS LONG AS SHE PAYS THE BILLS SHE WILL REMAIN THE BOSS.*

*NOTE: PRIOR TO THE MEETING TRACY WAS TOLD THAT SHE MUST TRAVEL TO NAPA VALLEY WITH MAX TODAY FOR A CONFERENCE THAT CINDY WAS TO OPEN TOMORROW. CINDY SAID SHE HAD BEEN INFORMED THAT HER HOME IS TO BE PICKETED*

*TOMORROW AND THEREFOR SHE DOES NOT FEEL SHE CAN BE OUT OF TOWN.*

*INTERESTING MORNING!!!!*

*OCTOBER 1, 1992*

*WELL, TODAY IS THE DAY! IF THE HENSLEYS FOLLOW THROUGH ON THEIR PLANS TODAY SHOULD BE THE DAY CINDY IS CONFRONTED ABOUT HER DEPENDENCY PROBLEM. I CERTAINLY HOPE FOR EVERYONE INVOLVED THAT THIS PROCESS WILL LEAD US TO HAPPIER TOMORROWS.*

*YESTERDAY WAS CERTAINLY INTERESTING. AFTER A STAFF MEETING IN WHICH CINDY LASHED OUT AT ALL OF US WHO MAKE AVMT HAPPEN SHE CALLED ME LAST NIGHT AT ALMOST 11:00 TO INFOR ME THAT MADONNA'S MOVIE "TRUTH OF DARE" WAS ON HBO. THE EXTREME SHIFTS IN MOOD WERE UNBELIEVABLE - IF I HAD NOT PERSONALLY WITNESSED THE SWINGS I WOULD NEVER BELIEVE THEM TO BE TRUE.*

*OCTOBER 2, 1992 - FRIDAY*

*WELL, IT IS DONE. LAST NIGHT JIM AND SMITTY CONFRONTED CINDY REGARDING HER DEPENDENCY TO PRESCRIPTION DRUGS AND SHE ADMITTED HER ADDICTION. I UNDERSTAND THAT SHE TOLD THE HENSLEYS HER ADDICTION WAS ROOTED IN HER UNHAPPINESS - HER MARRIAGE - AND THAT SHE TOOK PILLS TO MASK HER DEPRESSION. THE HENSLEYS TOLD CINDY THEY KNEW SHE HAD A PROBLEM BECAUSE OF HER SEVERE*

*MOOD SWINGS AND HER CHANGE IN CHARACTER. THE ALSO SAID HER MEANNESS TOWARDS OTHERS WAS NOT EXCUSABLE AND MUST STOP.*

*JIM HAS TOLD JERI THAT CINDY HAS A FEW DAYS TO TAKE CHARGE OF THE PROBLEM - IF SHE DOESN'T, THEY WILL CONTINUE TO PRESS THE ISSUE.*

*IT IS HARD TO SAY IF CINDY IS ON THE WAY TO RE-COVERY. A PERSON SO DISTURBED BY THEIR LIV-ING CONDITION MIGHT EITHER TAKE COMPLETE CONTROL OF THE SITUATION AND CORRECT IT OR THEY MIGHT GIVE APPEARANCES OF WORKING TO CORRECT THE PROBLEM WHILE IN REALITY THEY CONTINUE TO TAKE THE DRUGS IN A MUCH MORE CAREFUL AND SINISTER WAY. I HOPE FOR CINDY'S SAKE THAT SHE TAKES THE OPPORTUNITY HER PARENTS HAVE GIVEN HER TO CORRECT THE PROBLEM AND NOT ONLY GET OFF THE DRUGS BUT GETS RID OF THE EVEN GREATER UNDERLY-ING PROBLEM - HER MARRIAGE.*

*OCTOBER 2, 1992 - FRIDAY (SECOND ENTRY)*

*THE WORD IS, AT AVMT, THAT CINDY IS ON THE ROAD TO RECOVERY FROM HER BOUT WITH DRUGS. I THINK THE WORD COULD NOT BE FUR-THER FROM THE TRUTH.*

*FIRST OF ALL, CINDY IS VERY, VERY SHARP AND AL-THOUGH HER PARENTS MAY TINK THEY CAUGHT HER OFF GUARD I AM NOT SO SURE THAT SHE HASN'T ANTICIPATED THAT SOMEONE WOULD FIND OUT AND PREPARED HERSELF FOR THE CON-FRONTATION. SHE VERY SUCCESSFULLY MADE*

*THEM BELIEVE THAT HER UNHAPPY MARRIAGE IS THE CAUSE OF HER PROBLEM - THAT EXPLANATION BROUGHT A GREAT MOMENT OF SYMPATHY.  SECONDLY, CONSIDERING THE GREAT LENGTHS CINDY WENT TO OBTAIN HER SUPPLY I DO NOT BELIVE SHE WILL LET HER PLAN BE SO EASILY CHANGED.*

*AND THEN THERE IS THE KEN FACTOR.  HE WAS THE ONE PERSON CINDY SAW TODAY AND TOGETHER THEY DECIDED TO PRODUCE AN AVMT COMMEMORATIVE POSTER.  FOR WHAT?  UNLESS KEN CAN SHOW ME ON PAPER, BEYOND A REASONABLE DOUBT, THAT SUCH A PROPOSITION WILL CREATE A POSITIVE CASH FLOW I DO NOT FEEL AVMT SHOULD PURSUE IT.  REGARDLESS OF THE AMOUNT OF MONEY SUCH A PROMOTION GENERATES, KEN AKERS WILL BE PAID HIS DAILY RATE FOR PRODUCTION.  WHY NOT TIE KEN'S PAYMENT TO THE NET PROFIT OF THE SALE - AFTER ALL, HE STATES HE BELIEVES IN AVMT'S OBJECTIVE AND GOD KNOWS HE HAS MADE HIS FAIR SHARE OF MONEY FROM HIS DAILY RATE AND PRODUCTION COSTS OVER THE YEARS.*

*SO AM I PISSED?  YOU BET I AM.  AS IT NOT STANDS I DO NOT PLAY ANY ROLE AT AVMT OTHER THAN TO OBTAIN FREE OR REDUCED AIRLINE TICKETS, HANDLE THE LOGISTICS OF THE TEAM'S MOVEMENTS, AND SAY YES TO EVERY ASININE IDEA AND NOTION WHICH CINDY COOKS UP.*

*OCTOBER 5, 1992 - MONDAY*

*SO WHERE DO I BEGIN?*

*LAST FRIDAY, LATE IN THE AFTERNOON, MISS JERI WAS VISITING WITH DALTON SMITH, THE HENSLEYS' PILOT, ABOUT JIM AND SMITTY CONFRONTING CINDY ABOUT HER DRUG PROBLEM. DURING THE CONVERSATION DALTON MENTIONED AN INCIDENT WHICH TOOK PLACE A COUPLE OF YEARS AGO - CINDY HAD TAKEN TOO MANY PILLS AND HAD BEEN RUSHED TO A HOSPITAL NEAR THEIR HOME ON OAK CREEK. JOHN MCCAIN WAS RUSHED TO THE HOSPITAL AND RATHER THAN HELPING CINDY OBTAIN HELP HE HAD HER DISMISSED FROM THE HOSPITAL AND TAKEN TO THE CABIN. I HAD ASSUMED THE ENTIRE FAMILY KNEW OF THE INCIDENT AS KATHY WALKER HAD MENTIONED IT TO ME MANY MONTHS AGO BUT COME TO FIND OUT JERI AND THE HENSLEYS KNEW NOTHING OF IT. NEEDLESS TO SAY IT WAS VERY PAINFUL FOR MISS JERI TO FIND THIS OUT AND SHE WAS VERY CONCERNED ABOUT WHAT THE NEWS OF THIS OCCURRENCE WOULD DO TO JIM AND SMITTY. WHATEVER THE OUTCOME, I DOUBT THAT JIM AND SMITTY WILL EVER BE ABLE TO RESPECT JOHN MCCAIN AGAIN.*

*I REALLY DO NOT KNOW HOW TO REMOVE MYSELF FROM THIS SITUATION. I AM SO DEPENDENT ON MY INCOME FROM AVMT THAT I MUST STAY HERE UNTIL I FIND ANOTHER JOB. ALL OF THE CONFUSION CAUSED BY THIS CRAZINESS IS MAKING MY JOB ALMOST IMPOSSIBLE TO PERFORM. I DON'T KNOW IF I SHOULD SCHEDULE MEETINGS, I DON'T KNOW IF I SHOULD COMMIT THE ORGANIZATION WHICH IT MIGHT NOT BE ABLE TO FULFILL, AND I DON'T KNOW FROM DAY-TO-DAY IF I HAVE ANY JOB SECURITY ON WHICH I CAN DEPEND.*

*BASED ON MY TENURE WITH AVMT I AM NOT COMFORTABLE BELIEVING I WOULD BE OF-FERED ANY SEVERANCE PACKAGE SHOULD CINDY CHOOSE TO DISMISS ME. THE HENSLEYS HAVE SO MUCH MONEY THEY COULD EASILY SMASH ME SHOULD I CHOOSE TO PURSUE LEGAL ACTION - CINDY USED MY NAME WHEN ORDERING DRUGS FROM PROFESSIONAL WITHOUT MY KNOWLEDGE OF THE TRANSACTION - I BELIEVE THAT IS FRAUD.*

*SATURDAY I WENT TO THE HENSLEY & COMPANY PICNIC AT A PARK NEAR MY HOME. DIDN'T STAY LONG AS I NEVER FEEL A PART OF THAT ORGANI-ZATION. VISITED A BIT WITH KATHY WALKER AND HER GIRLS - ALSO SAW TRACY ORRICK AND LARRY, HER BOYFRIEND. MY RELATIONSHIP WITH TRACY HAS BEEN STRAINED BECAUSE OF CINDY'S POOR MANAGEMENT OF AVMT. I FEEL BAD THAT TRACY AND I DO NOT GET ALONG AS WE SHOULD BUT AS LONG AS CINDY CONTINUES TO MANAGE AVMT BY PHONE, ALL OF US FEEL THE STRAINS OF A LESS-THAN-IDEAL WORK ENVIRONMENT.*

*OCTOBER 6, 1992 - TUESDAY*

*ALL SHIT HIT THE FAN YESTERDAY!*

*JERI JOHNSON CALLED DR MOFFO TO ASK HIM NOT TO FILL ANYMORE PRESCRIPTIONS FOR CINDY MCCAIN. DR MOFFO SAID HE HAD NOT BEEN FILLING ANY PRESCRIPTIONS FOR CINDY - IT SEEMS CINDY HAS BEEN USING TOM'S DEA NUM-BER TO OBTAIN HER DRUGS.*

*JIM HENSLEY CALLED CINDY THIS MORNING AND TOLD HER NOT TO USE MOFFO'S NUMBER AGAIN. SHE DENIED SHE HAD USED THE NUMBER AND SINCE THEN HAS BEEN TRYING TO CONTACT MOFFO. GOD KNOWS WHAT SHE WILL SAY TO MOFFO IF SHE REACHES HIM. ALSO, CINDY WAS TRYING TO REACH DR JOHN JOHNSON. SHE IS EITHER TRYING TO DO SOME QUICK DAMAGE CONTROL OR SHE IS GOING TO SET SOMEBODY UP FOR THE FALL.*

*AS CINDY WAS NOT ABLE TO CONTACT DR MOFFO SHE ALSO HAD KEN AKERS, HER PHOTOGRAPHER AND CONFIDANT, TRY AND REACH TOM. AS FAR AS I KNOW TOM HAS NOT YET RECEIVED KEN'S CALL.*

*WHAT ARE WE TO DO? I REALLY WANT OUT OF THIS MESS. IT IS IMPOSSIBLE FOR ME TO GET ANYTHING DONE. I HAVE JUST RECENTLY COME TO REALIZE HOW WICKED AND CALCULATED CINDY MCCAIN CAN BE - WHO KNOWS WHAT SHE WILL DO TO COVER UP THIS MESS AND WHOM SHE WILL TRY AND PUT THE BLAME ON.*

*KATHY IS SICK OF IT. TRACY IS SICK OF IT. JERI IS SICK OF IT. AND GOD KNOW, I AM SICK OF IT.*

*OCTOBER 7, 1992 - WEDNESDAY*

*MORE OF THE SAME.*

*YESTERDAY THE MOFFO ISSUE BECAME MORE COMPLICATED. AFTER JIM HENSLEY CONFRONTED CINDY WITH INFORMATION ABOUT HER USING TOM'S NAME TO OBTAIN DRUGS CINDY*

*CALLED MOFFO TO QUESTION HIM. MOFFO TOLD CINDY HE WOULD NOT DO ANY FOLLOW UP, IE, TURN HER IN, BUT TOLD HER TO NEVER DO IT AGAIN.*

*THIS MORNING CINDY CALLED ME TO INFORM ME THAT SHE AND MAX JOHNSON HAD CONTACTED THE DEA AND ASKED THAT AN INVESTIGATION BE CONDUCTED TO "INVESTIGATE ALLEGATIONS MADE AGAINST HER". SHE SAID A "BOGUS" PHONE CALL HAD BEEN RECEIVED WHICH MADE WILD ACCUSATIONS ABOUT HER AND THAT SHE BE-LIEVED THE PHONE CALL WAS "POLITICAL". CIN-DY ALSO SAID SHE HAD CALLED THE SUPPOSED ORIGINATOR OF THE CALL AND THAT THE INDI-VIDUAL DENIED EVER MAKING THE CALL.*

*NO TIME DURING HER DISCUSSION WITH ME DID CINDY STATE DR TOM MOFFO'S NAME.*

*CINDY WENT ON TO STATE THAT KATHY WOULD BE ACCOMPANYING MAX JOHNSON TO THE DEA THIS AFTERNOON TO DISPOSE OF DRUGS IN AVMT'S POSSESSION. SHE AGAIN STATED THAT SHE HAD ASKED FOR A FOLLOWUP INVESTIGA-TION OF THE ACCUSATIONS OF YESTERDAY.*

*OCTOBER 9, 1992 - FRIDAY*

*THE PAST COUPLE OF DAYS HAVE BEEN RELATIVELY QUIET - CINDY HAS BEEN OUT OF TOWN WITH JOHN. WE ARE ALL STILL QUITE DISTURBED THAT SHE WOULD EVEN SUGGEST TO DR MAX JOHNSON THAT DR MOFFO HAS A DRUG PROBLEM WHEN IN REALITY WE ALL KNOW*

*THAT SHE IS THE PERSON WHO USED DR MOFFO'S NAME TO GET THE DRUGS TO WHICH SHE HAS BECOME ADDICTED. I HOPE THAT CINDY HAS THE GOOD SENSE NOT TO SAY ANYTHING MORE TO DR JOHNSON, MEMBERS OF THE AVMT STAFF, OR DOCTOR AND INDIVIDUALS OUTSIDE THE ORGANIZATION - ANYTHING MORE SAID COULD PROVOKE DR MOFFO.*

*WORK CONTINUES TO BE A CHALLENGE. TRACY STILL DOESN'T UNDERSTAND HOW IMPORTANT IT IS TO COMMUNICATE. SHE IS REALLY PRETTY STUPIC WHEN IT COMES TO OFFICE POLITICS AND DEALING WITHIN THIS ORGANIZATION SPECIFI-CALLY. I WOULD LIKE TO THINK HER INABILITY TO FIGURE THINGS OUT IS DUE TO HER INEXPE-RIENCE BUT I AM BECOMING MORE AND MORE AWARE THAT SHE IS SIMPLY NOT VERY BRIGHT. RATHER THAN CONTINUE TO TRU AND WORK WITH HER I HAVE DECIDED IT IS TIME TO LET HER FALL ON HER FACE.*

*OCTOBER 22, 1992 - THURSDAY*

*LAST THURSDAY HAD TO BE ONE OF THE MOST INTERESTING DAYS I HAVE HAD AROUND HERE IN A LONG TIME. EARLY THURSDAY AFTERNOON CINDY MCCAIN CALLED TO TALK ABOUT BRIDGET MCCAIN'S ADOPTION HEARING WHICH WAS TO BE HELD THE NEXT DAY. CINDY STATED THAT SOMEWHERE, BRENDAY CHURCH, CINDY'S AT-TORNEY FOR THE CASE HAD GOTTEN THE IDEA THAT BRIDGET'S FATHER WAS DEAD AND THAT I SHOULD JUST PLAY ALONG WITH HER GAME PLAN.*

*FOLLOWING MY CONVERSATION WITH CINDY
I WAS CONTACTED BY MELINDA GRAYSON, A
YOUNG ATTORNEY WHO WAS REPLACING BRENDA
CHURCN AS BRENDA HAD BEEN ADMITTED TO
THE HOSPITAL EARLIER IN THE WEEK FOR AN
APPENDICITIS. MELINDA ASKED ME SEVERAL
QUESTIONS ABOUT MY TRIPS TO BANGLADESH
(BRIDGET'S HOME) AND WHAT KNOWLEDGE I HAD
OF THE BIRTH PARENTS. I TOLD MELINDA THAT I
HAD SEEN THE MOTHER WHEN I WAS IN DHAKA IN
JUNE AND THAT I HAD BEEN TOLD THAT THE FA-
THER HAD VANISHED, DISAPPEARED - NEVER DID I
HEAR THE WORD DEAD USED BY THE MOTHER OR
THE NUNS AT THE ORPHANAGE.*

*AFTER TALKING TO MELINDA I DECIDED THAT
CINDY HAD OBVIOUSLY MADE UP SOME CRAZY
STORY ABOUT BRIDGET'S FATHER AND THAT SHE
WAS ABOUT TO INVOLVE ME IN THE LIE. SO, I
CALLED CINDY BACK AND STATED THAT I WAS
VERY UNCOMFORTABLE SAYING THE FATHER WAS
DEAD, THAT WE WOULD BE TESTIFYING UNDER
OATH AND THAT I WOULD NOT LIE. CINDY TOLD
ME THAT I SHOULD DO WHAT WAS RIGHT.*

*I CALLED MELINDA AGAIN. DURING THIS CALL I
TOLD MELINDA THAT SINCE I WOULD BE TESTI-
FYING UNDER OAT I WOULD NOT USE THE WORD
DEAD BUT THAT I WOULD ONLY USE THE WORDS
THE NUNS HAD USED IN THEIR TRANSLATION -
VANISHED, DISAPPEARED.*

*AND THE THE STRANGEST TWIST TO THE TALE
OCCURRED - MELINDA ASKED WHAT I KNOW
ABOUT THE RICKSHAW ACCIDENT. MY RESPONSE*

*- WHAT RICKSHAW ACCIDENT? MELINDA TOLD ME THAT CINDY HAD STATED IN HER SWORN DEPOSITION THAT BRIDGET'S FATHER HAD BEEN KILLED IN A RICKSHAW ACCIDENT. NEEDLESS TO SAY I WAS SHOCKED BY THE NEWS BUT NOT IN DISBELIEF AS I ALSO KNOW THAT THE SOURCE OF THIS INFORMATION IS A HABITUAL LIAR.*

*WELL, THE HEARING WENT FINE - CINDY LIED UNDER OATH STATING SHE HAD HEARD OF THE FATHER'S UNFORTUNATE DEATH. I WAS ASKED QUESTIONS WHICH DID NOT REQUIRE THAT I USE THE WORD DEAD OR DEATH. THE JUDGE WAS TOTALLY TAKEN IN BY CINDY'S PRESENCE AND THE MESSAGE AND RULED IN HER FAVOR. CHALK ANOTHER ONE UP FOR CINDY.*

*BEYOND THE THURSDAY AND FRIDAY HAPPENINGS I WENT TO THE STATE FAIR WITH CINDY, A NANNY AND THE KIDS ON MONDAY. REGARDLESS OF WHAT I THINK OF CINDY, I THINK THE KIDS ARE GREAT AND WOULD DO ANYTHING FOR THEM.*

*TRACY TOLD ME TODAY THAT CINDY AGREED TO GIVE HER A RAISE. I AM NOT UPSET THAT TRACY IS GETTING A RAISE BUT I AM UPSET THAT I HAVE BEEN OVERLOOKED AND THAT MY ACTUAL CONTRIBUTION TO THE ORGANIZATION IS GREATER THAN HERS. THE FACT THAT I WAS OVERLOOKED IS NOT TRACY'S FAULT, IT IS CINDY'S FOR NOT REVIEWING MY PROGRESS.*

*OCTOBER 28, 1992 - WEDNESDAY*

*THE PAST WEEK HAS BEEN PRETTY QUIET. CINDY MCCAIN HAS BEEN BUSY CAMPAIGNING - IT IS LESS THAN A WEEK UNTIL THE ELECTIONS - SO SHE HASN'T BEEN AROUND TO MAKE OUR LIVES MORE COMPLICATED THAN THEY NEED TO BE. WITH THE EXCEPTION OF AN OCCASIONAL PHONE CALL I DON'T ANTICIPATE THAT WE WILL HEAR FROM CINDY BETWEEN NOW AND THE NEW YEAR - FOLLOWING THE ELECTION SHE AND JOHN BEGIN A SERIES OF RATHER LENGTHY VACATIONS.*

*WORK CONTINUES TO BE AS STUPID AND NON-PROFESSIONAL AS USUAL. YESTERDAY I MADE THE SUGGESTION THAT IT WOULD BE NICE IF THE TYPE STYLE OF THE AVMT CALENDAR BE CONSIS-TENT WITH THAT USED ON OUR LETTERHEAD AND BUSINESS CARDS. WELL, WAS THAT A MISTAKE. KEN AKERS, CINDY'S PHOTOGRAPHER, FRIEND, TOY (AND I MIGHT ADD A RATHER SOCIALLY INEPT IN-DIVIDUAL) HAD ALREADY STARTED PRODUCTION OF THE CALENDAR. HE STATED THAT IF THERE WERE TO BE ANY CHANGES HE WOULD TAKE OR-DERS FROM CINDY ONLY. SO MUCH FOR ME EVER WORKING WITH KEN AKERS AGAIN.*

*I AM STILL CONCERNED ABOUT CINDY MCCAIN'S DRUG PROBLEM - IT SEEMS HER PARENTS ARE FALLING INTO A DENIAL MODE AND BELIEVE THAT TIME WILL HEAL CINDY'S PROBLEM. I REAL-LY DON'T BELIVE THAT IS POSSIBLE - CINDY IS SO FAR GONE THAT IF SOMEONE DOESN'T HELP HER SOON SHE WILL EITHER KILL HERSELF OR MORE SERIOUSLY, RISH THE SAFETY OF HER FAMILY*

*WHILE UNDER THE INFLUENCE OF THE DRUGS. I CAN'T EVEN BEGIN TO IMAGINE WHAT THE OUTCOME WILL BE - I AM VERY CONCERNED FOR EVERYONE INVOLVED.*
*NOVEMBER 3, 1992 - TUESDAY*

*WORK IS VERY SLOW. YESTERDAY I BEGAN CALLING PROSPECTIVE DONORS TO ASK FOR FIVE YEAR PLEDGES - IT IS IMPORTANT THAT AVMT HAVE SOME IDEA OF WHAT ITS FUTURE CASH FLOW WILL BE. I THINK MY JOB MAY HINGE ON MY ABILITY TO RAISE CASH FOR THE ORGANIZATION EVEN THOUGH THAT WAS NOT INTENDED TO BE MY MAIN FUNCTION.*

*TONIGHT I AM ATTENDING AN ELECTION RESULTS PARTY AT THE MCCAIN'S HOME - MIA TSANG IS GOING AS MY DATE. JOHN IS EXPECTED TO WIN HIS RACE BY A LANDSLIDE BUT I DON'T THINK THE REST OF THE REPUBLICAN PARTY WILL FAIR AS WELL. THIS HAS REALLY BEEN A TURBULENT POLITICAL YEAR - I HAVE CERTAINLY HAD MIXED EMOTIONS ABOUT DIFFERENT RACES.*

*NOVEMBER 25, 1992 - WEDNESDAY*

*CINDY AND JOHN MCCAIN HAVE BEEN OUT OF TOWN FOR THE PAST FEW WEEKS SO WORK HAS BEEN WONDERFUL. WHEN CINDY IS OUT OF TOWN WORK IS UNBELIEVABLY CALM AND MANAGEABLE - DAYS GO BY WITHOUT ANY EARTH SHAKING EVENTS AND EVERYONE IN THE OFFICE SEEMS TO GET ALONG MUCH BETTER AND DO NOT SEEM TO BE PITTED AGAINST ONE ANOTHER LIKE THEY ARE WHEN CINDY IS IN TOWN.*

*HOWEVER, WHEN SHE RETURNS THE CIRCUS BEGINS ANEW.*

*DECEMBER 22, 1992 - TUESDAY*

*FIRST OF ALL, WORK! AVMT CONTINUES TO PLUG ALONG WITHOUT DIRECTION OR LEADERSHIP. CINDY HAS CREATED A TOTALLY DYSFUNCTIONAL STAFF - KATHY IS A PUPPER TO HER EVERY WHIM, JER IS A MESS (THE PRODUCT OF SEVERAL IN-FAMILY SQUABBLES) AND TRACY HASN'T HAD ENOUGH EXPERIENCE TO UNDERSTAND WHAT A STRANGE PLACE AVMT IS TO WORK.*

*I HAVE MIXED EMOTIONS ABOUT WHAT I BELIEVE SHOULD HAPPEN TO AVMT. IT DOES NOT DESERVE TO CONTINUE TO EXIST AS IT IS CURRENTLY BEING OPERATED - IT IS A VERY EXPENSIVE TOY FOR A VERY DISTURBED LADY. CINDY HAS USED THE ORGANIZATION FOR SELF-PROMOTION AND AS A SOURCE FOR THE DRUGS TO WHICH SHE IS ADDICTED. I HAD REALLY THOUGHT THAT EITHER HER MOTHER OR FATHER WOULD FORCE HER INTO TREATMENT BUT AS THE DAYS, WEEKS, AND MONTHS PASS I AM NOT CONFIDENT THAT WILL OCCUR. CINDY CONTINUES TO EITHER PERSUADE DOCTORS THAT THE LARGE QUANTITIES OF DRUGS SHE ORDERS ARE TO BE SHIPPED TO THIRD WORLD COUNTRIES OR SHE MUST BE USING THEIR NAMES AND DEA NUMBERS TO OBTAIN THE DRUGS WITHOUT THEIR KNOWLEDGE OF IT.*

*THE MCCAIN FAMILY - WHAT A SCREWED UP MESS. LAST WEEK CINDY AND HER ADOPTED DAUGHTER*

*CARI HAD A MAJOR ARGUMENT. THE RESULT FOUND CARI BANNED FROM THE MCCAIN HOME, CUT OFF FINANCIALLY AND LIVING WITH HER GRANDMOTHER. BEYOND THAT, CARI FLUNKED HER FIRST SEMESTER IN COLLEGE AND JUST THIS SATURDAY, ONE DAY FOLLOWING THE MCCAIN'S DEPARTURE FOR TURTLE ISLAND, BECAME ENGAGED TO FRANK BRABEC, A PREMED STUDENT WHO TRAVELED TO KUWAIT AND BANGLADESH WITH AVMT. GOD HELP US ALL WHEN CINDY GETS NEWS OF THE ENGAGEMENT.*

*THE REST OF THE STORY. JERI JOHNSON HAD A MILD STROKE LAST THURSDAY - THE STRESS WAS TOO MUCH FOR HER.*

*JANUARY 11, 1993 - MONDAY*

*CINDY WAS IN THE OFFICE TODAY - FIRST TIME IN A COUPLE OF MONTHS.*

*SHE AND I MET WITH JOHN BIRCUMSHAW TO DIS-CUSS AN APRIL FUNDRAISER AND JOHN'S GRANT WRITING EFFORTS. SHORTLY AFTER THE MEET-ING, CINDY, VERY CASUALLY, TOLD ME THAT I WON'T BE TRAVELING TO CALCUTTA NEXT WEEK, INSTEAD I AM TO STAY IN PHOENIX AND WORK ON THE NAVAJO NATION PROJECT. GOD ONLY KNOWS WHAT ALL OF THIS MEANS.*

*I WANT TO LEAVE AVMT AS SOON AS POSSIBLE - CINDY MCCAIN AND HER BIZARRE, DRUG IN-DUCED BEHAVIOR IS MORE THAN I CAN HANDLE. I DON'T KNOW WHEN I HAVE EVER MET A PERSON WHO IS MORE SCREWED UP THAT SHE IS - IF SHE*

*DIDN'T HAVE MONEY BEHIND HER SHE WOULD BE
A COMPLETE MESS.*

*ETHICALLY I HAVE MIXED FEELINGS ABOUT MY
RESPONSIBILITIES TO AVMT AND TH DOCTORS
WHO HAVE INNOCENTLY AND UNKNOWINGLY
BEEN INVOLVED IN CINDY'S PROBLEM. I THINK
ABOUT IT DAILY.*

*JANUARY 12, 1993 - TUESDAY*

*YESTERDAY TURNED OUT TO BE A VERY GOOD
DAY - NOT BECAUSE I WAS ABLE TO CHANGE ANY-
THING AT AVMT BUT BECAUSE I REALIZED IF I
WANT CHANGE I WILL HAVE TO MAKE IT HAPPEN.*

*TODAY I ARRIVED AT THE OFFICE CALM AND CON-
FIDENT IN KNOWING THAT THE BEST THING I
CAN DO FOR MYSELF IS FIND A NEW JOB. IT IS EV-
IDENT THAT I WILL NOT INFLUENCE THE FUTURE
OF AVMT - AS LONG AS CINDY CONTROLS THE
PURSE STRINGS THE ORGANIZATION'S FUTURE
WILL CONTINUE TO TRAVEL ALONG THE SAME
BUMPY ROAD ON WHICH IT HAS ALWAYS TRAV-
ELED - BUT I CAN CHANGE MY WORK SITUATION
BY MAINTAINING A POSITIVE ATTITUDE AND AG-
GRESSIVELY SEEKING NEW EMPLOYMENT. THE
NEGATIVE EFFECT AVMT HAS HAD ON ME HAS
BEEN MONUMENTAL AND ONLY I CAN TURN THAT
AROUND AND MAKE MYSELF A STRONGER PERSON
BECAUSE OF IT.*

*THERE ARE MANY LESSONS I HAVE LEARNED
FROM WORK WITH CINDY MCAIN: ASK CURRENT
AND FORMER EMPLOYEES ABOUT THE WORKING*

*ENVIRONMENT; DETERMINE IF THE EMPLOYER'S ACTIONS ARE SINCERE OR OTHERWISE MOTIVATED; BE CAREFUL NOT TO BE TAKEN IN BY PROMISES OF ADVANCEMENT AND REWARD; AND STUDY BODY LANGUAGE - LACK OF EYE CONTACT, NAIL BITING, AND BLOTCHY SKIN MIGHT BE SIGNS OF UNEASINESS AND DISHONESTY.*

*CINDY HAS TURNED OUT TO BE A VERY INTEREST-ING PERSON TO STUDY. WHEN SHE IS IN CASUAL, NONTHREATENING ENVIRONMENTS SHE CAN BE VERY NICE AND FUN TO BE WITH. HOWEVER, WHEN SHE IS IN A DEPRESSED MOOD OR IN UN-COMFORTABLE ENVIRONMENTS SHE BECOMES IR-RATIONAL AND CONFRONTATIONAL.*

*I DON'T KNOW WHAT CINDY'S PROBLEMS STEM FROM AND IT IS VERY UNFORTUNATE FOR HER THAT BECAUSE OF HER POSITION AND WEALTH SHE HAS NEVER BEEN FORCED TO DEAL WITH THEM. I FEEL SORRY FOR CINDY THAT SO MANY PEOPLE ARE AWARE OF HER OBVIOUS PROBLEMS - DRUG ABUSE AND PATHOLOGICAL LYING - AND ARE UNWILLING OR UNABLE TO HELP HER. EV-ERYONE AROUND HER HAS BEEN, IN SOME WAY, EFFECTED BYHER OUTBURSTS YET NO ONE HAS EVER DARED QUESTION HER ABOUT THEM.*

*IN THE PAST EIGHTEEN MONTHS I HAVE SEEN CINDY TAKE ON SO MANY DIFFERENT PERSONALI-TIES THAT I CAN NO LONGER IDENTIFY WHEN SHE IS PLAYING ROLE FROM WHEN SHE IS BEING SINCERE.*

*JANUARY 13, 1993 - WEDNESDAY*

*CHALK UP ANOTHER DAY AT AVMT.*

*YESTERDAY WAS GOING GREAT UNTIL I GOT A CALL FROM CINDY MCCAIN WHO STATED THAT SHE HEARD I WAS MAD BECAUSE I WASN'T GOING TO INDIA.*

*I EXPLAINED TO CINDY THAT WHEN SHE TOLD ME I WAS NOT GOING TO BE TRAVELING TO CAL-CUTTA I WAS UPSET BECAUSE OF THE INCON-VENIENCE THAT THE LAST MINUTE CHANGE IN PLANS HAD CAUSED - I HAD DECLINED INVITA-TIONS FOR THE NEXT WEEK AND HAD MADE AR-RANGEMENTS TO HAVE MY HOUSE WATCH. I ALSO TOLD CINDY THAT AFTER I HAD TAKEN TIME TO DIGEST THE CHANGE IN PLANS I DECIDED I WAS, IN FACT, RELIEVED THAT I WOULD NOT BE TRAV-ELING TO CALCUTTA AND THAT I HAD ALREADY SCHEDULED MEETINGS FOR NEXT WEEK.*

*IT IS EVIDENT TO ME THAT AVMT IS IN SERIOUS NEED OF AN ORGANIZATIONAL CHANGE. IT IS IMPOSSIBLE FOR ANYONE TO MANAGE A BUSI-NESS OVER THE PHONE WHEN THOSE WHO ARE PHYSICALLY LOCATED AT THE OFFICE HAVE NOT BEEN GRANTED ANY FORM OF AUTHORITY OR RESPONSIBILITY. OUR SHOT GUM APPROACH TO PROVIDING MEDICAL CARE HAS MINIMAL IMPACE WHEN A FOCUSED APPROACH ON A SPECIFIC ARE OR TYPE OF CARE COULD SIGNIFICANTLY IMPACT THE TARGET CONSTITUENCY.*

*IN DISCUSSING CINDY'S PHONE CALL, KATHY AND I DETERMINED THAT TRACY EITHER TOLD CINDY DIRECTLY OR SHE TOLD KEN AKERS WHO THEN TOLD CINDY THAT I WAS UPSET BY THE CHANGE OF PLANS.*

*JANUARY 15, 1993 - FRIDAY*

*WELL YESTERDAY WAS CERTAINLY A BANG!*

*FOR THE FIRST TIME IN MY LIFE I WAS FIRED FROM A JOB. CINDY ASKED ME TO COME TO HER OFFICE SO THAT WE MIGHT SPEAK. SHE IMMEDIATELY HANDED ME A TERMINATION LETTER AND BEGAN A SPEECH OF PRAISE. SHE THANKED ME FOR MY CONTRIBUTION TO AVMT, FOR MY LOYALTY AND STATED SHE WOULD BE "FOREVER THANKFUL" FOR WHAT I HAD DONE FOR HER NEWEST DAUGHTER, BRIDGET MCCAIN.*

*END OF CHAPTER.*

Made in the USA
Charleston, SC
27 August 2013